THE
WORLD
IN RIPENESS

ALSO BY H. E. BATES

Novels

THE TWO SISTERS

CHARLOTTE'S ROW

THE POACHER

SPELLA HO

THE CRUISE OF THE BREADWINNER

THE JACARANDA TREE

LOVE FOR LYDIA

THE SLEEPLESS MOON

THE DARLING BUDS OF MAY

A BREATH OF FRENCH AIR

A CROWN OF WILD MYRTLE

THE DISTANT HORNS OF SUMMER

CATHERINE FOSTER

THE FALLOW LAND

A HOUSE OF WOMEN

FAIR STOOD THE WIND FOR FRANCE

THE PURPLE PLAIN

THE SCARLET SWORD

THE FEAST OF JULY

WHEN THE GREEN WOODS LAUGH

THE DAY OF THE TORTOISE

OH! TO BE IN ENGLAND

A MOMENT IN TIME

A LITTLE OF WHAT YOU FANCY

THE TRIPLE ECHO (*Illustrated by Ron Clarke*)

Short Stories

DAY'S END

THE BLACK BOXER

CUT AND COME AGAIN

THE FLYING GOAT

THE BRIDE COMES TO EVENSFORD

COLONEL JULIAN

THE WATERCRESS GIRL

DEATH OF A HUNTSMAN

THE GOLDEN ORIOLE

THE WILD CHERRY TREE

SEVEN TALES AND ALEXANDER

THE WOMAN WHO HAD

    IMAGINATION

SOMETHING SHORT AND SWEET

THE BEAUTY OF THE DEAD

DEAR LIFE

THE DAFFODIL SKY

NOW SLEEPS THE CRIMSON PETAL

THE NATURE OF LOVE

AN ASPIDISTRA IN BABYLON

THE FOUR BEAUTIES

THE SONG OF THE WREN

Drama

THE DAY OF GLORY

Essays

FLOWERS AND FACES

DOWN THE RIVER

THE HEART OF THE COUNTRY

THE COUNTRY HEART

THROUGH THE WOODS

THE SEASONS AND THE GARDENER

O! MORE THAN HAPPY COUNTRYMAN

THE COUNTRY OF WHITE CLOVER

EDWARD GARNETT: A MEMOIR

Collections of Short Stories

THIRTY TALES

THE FABULOUS MRS V.

COUNTRY TALES

MY UNCLE SILAS

(*Illustrated by Edward Ardizzone*)

THE WEDDING PARTY

SEVEN BY FIVE

SUGAR FOR THE HORSE

(*Illustrated by Edward Ardizzone*)

Criticism

THE MODERN SHORT STORY

Autobiography

THE VANISHED WORLD

(*Illustrated by John Ward*)

THE BLOSSOMING WORLD

(*Illustrated by John Ward*)

As 'Flying Officer X'

THE GREATEST PEOPLE IN THE WORLD   HOW SLEEP THE BRAVE

For Children

ACHILLES THE DONKEY   ACHILLES AND DIANA

H. E. BATES

THE
WORLD
IN RIPENESS

An Autobiography

VOLUME THREE

Illustrated by John Ward

LONDON
MICHAEL JOSEPH

First published in Great Britain by
MICHAEL JOSEPH LTD
52 Bedford Square
London, W.C.1
1972

The quotation from
Overture for Beginners
by R. F. Delderfield is printed
by kind permission of
Hodder & Stoughton Ltd

Set and printed in Great Britain by Tonbridge Printers Ltd, Peach Hall Works, Tonbridge, Kent, in Baskerville eleven on thirteen point on paper supplied by P. F. Bingham Ltd and bound by James Burn at Esher, Surrey

I

Burdened by an impossibly large and heavy blue cabin trunk, I set off on October 17, 1941, for the Royal Air Force Station at Uxbridge, there to engage in a three-week Officers' Training Course. The afternoon was utterly typical of an English mid-October: the air limpid, soft and warm as new milk, the distances touched with that same tender haze that must surely have inspired Keats' 'Season of mists and mellow fruitfulness'.

I only wish I could say the same for my own spirits; but I fear that for all my natural buoyancy, it was not so. Honoured though I was to have been singled out by Air Ministry to be the first writer ever to be commissioned in the Armed Forces solely as a writer of short stories I must nevertheless confess to having been slightly heavy of heart. I was leaving behind me a young wife, who had somehow to manage, on God only knew how little money, to feed and clothe and comfort four children under the age of eight, in a part of England where, even though the immediate threat of German invasion had receded, constant day and night raids by enemy bombers and fighters were still very much part of the day's unamusing routine.

I could, I think, have dodged this particular column, largely on the grounds that Officers' Training Courses do not have, as part of their curriculum, any special instructional periods for the guidance of short story writers; but I was determined in this, as in other matters, to seek no special favours, and I have ever since been specially glad that I did not do so.

The scene at Uxbridge was in part comic, in part sad. It rather resembled one of those appalling Old Boys' Reunions at which some men remember others only too well whereas others, either by design or the sheer passage of years, have forgotten. ('By God, it's old Jonesy. Remember? Upper Fifth. 1922. Gosh, you were a devil. Remember how you set fire to your Latin crib one day? Just got the damn thing burning merrily when the Old Man himself popped in. God! – talk about laugh! Remember?') Some, as I say, remembered; some, on the contrary, did not. An air of uneasy embarrassment hung over everything as the extraordinary motley company of players attempted to sort out their baggage, find their billets and beds and somehow accustom themselves to the thought of a sort of semi-monastic three-weeks' imprisonment.

Shop-keepers, schoolmasters, small business men, hoteliers, solicitors, commercial travellers, engineers, clerks, accountants: motley, indeed, the assembly was. Most were family men in their early or mid thirties. One was a Rugby International; another, rather fat and podgy, appeared to have been honoured with some special dispensation, since he wore on his sleeve not the miserable thin blue line that is the mark of the lowly entrant Pilot Officer, but the huge broad ring that denotes none other than the lofty Air Commodore. All of us treated this

particular gentleman not only with awe and respect but a certain suspicion that he had been placed among us as a sort of guardian-cum-spy. It was not until next day that we discovered he had, unfortunately, suffered from the misguidance of an over-zealous tailor.

That night fifty or so of us were herded together as in a school dormitory. The atmosphere was in keeping; there was much farting; I slept badly. In the morning, by now turned alarmingly chilly, we paraded at an ungodly hour for the customary injection against small-pox, tetanus and so on. One of my companion officers had turned out to be an old schoolfellow, also a Rugby player, a hefty young man of some fifteen or sixteen stone. He was behind me in the queue for jabs. Suddenly I was stunned by a sound as of falling masonry and turned to see my erstwhile schoolmate flat on his back, cold and glassy-eyed.

Soon we were being addressed, in terms alternately avuncular, soothing and stern, by the Commanding Officer, who solemnly assured us that, as if we were about to enter Holy Orders, the RAF Officers' Training Course, Uxbridge, could bring nothing but physical, mental, moral and indeed spiritual elevation to our wretched and all too recently civilian souls. We listened in silence, as yet unconverted.

Presently we were led, with a sort of casual subtlety, into the curriculum itself. This consisted of a couple of hours' square-bashing after breakfast, followed by a short break, then followed by a lecture and then, after lunch, by a further lecture and more square-bashing. I didn't really mind the square-bashing; at least, on the suddenly freezing October days, it kept the blood in circulation. Of the lectures it is hard to say if they were worse than the lecturers; but on balance I should, in memory, vote slightly in the lectures' favour, little though that may mean.

One of the lecturers was a kind of stage silly ass type commonly seen in those appalling musical comedies of the 1920s; dapper and la-di-da of voice, he conceived it stupendously clever to enliven his sessions with *risqué* stories having neither point nor humour (*A Waaf had an accident; she fell out of bed. She was*

7

swerving to avoid a child), at the same time offering us not a single improving word. Another was an ex-public school master of infinite and lofty snobbery whose constant injunction to us was 'always to remember our *Alma Mater*'. A third was a semi-illiterate whose favourite word was *personnel*, pronounced roughly to rhyme with *Rommel*. I used to listen to him, I fear, half-shrouded in sleep.

It must have been on the second or third day of the course that I fell in with an ex-hotelier from Cornwall who had earned his commission the hard way, having come up from the ranks. As a result there was nothing, absolutely nothing, that he didn't know about dodging duties, responsibilities and parades, bending or breaking the rules, always quite legitimately, and generally avoiding the harsher moments of service life. My first experience of these long-acquired ingenuities occurred on a frigid afternoon when thin flakes of snow were dismally floating through the darkening air, making the thought of an afternoon parade, without overcoats, more than a slightly forbidding one. Duty bound, spruced and ready, I was nevertheless about to leave the dormitory when to my infinite astonishment I saw my friend the hotelier lying indolently on his bed, still in his shirt sleeves. The following conversation then took place.

'It's two o'clock already. Hadn't you better get ready for parade?'

'Not coming.'

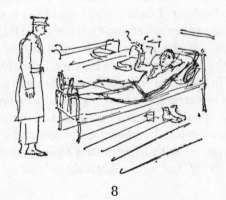

'*Not coming?*'

'No.'

'Good God, why ever not?'

'Going out.'

'*Going out?* Where on earth to?'

'Dental.'

This single cryptic word was drenched with all the distillation of long experience. Dental? Was there, I enquired, something wrong with my friend's teeth? Had he toothache?

'No.'

'Then if there's nothing wrong with your teeth why are you going to dental?'

'Well of course there might be something wrong that I don't know about and of course I shan't know, shall I, until I get the dentist to have a look? I'll be back for tea.'

The next afternoon, again snatched prematurely from winter, the word 'dental' was replaced by 'medical'. When I inquired if my friend was feeling ill he airily replied that, on the contrary, he felt as fit as a fiddle. But that didn't mean, did it, that there might not be something wrong and until you got the doctor to have a look you couldn't know, could you?

The following evening he proceeded to announce a still more audacious piece of adventure. He was going to town for the night. He had, it seemed, a pleasant little bird up there.

'But Good God, man, you can't be out of camp all night.'

'Oh! yes, I can.'

'But have you a special pass or something?'

'Don't need one. As long as you're on parade at eight-thirty next morning you can do what the hell you like with your nights.'

'But I thought we were supposed to stay in and swot up King's Regulations and all that, ready for the passing-out exam.'

'All baloney. What's the point of swotting up when you're allowed to take all your notes into the exam? What's the point of reading King's Regulations when you've got all the answers anyway?'

9

'I never thought of that.'

'Well, you must, old boy, you must. Listen to me. Never be too bloody diligent and all that. If you are they'll spot it like a hawk and have you posted to some Hell-hole like Aden or somewhere. That's where they send the nice, good, obedient types. Not my sort. They know we can't be trusted.'

'You amaze me.'

'Glad to hear it, old boy. And let me tell you something else. *Never be on time anywhere.* Whenever you're posted always turn up a couple of days late. Why? A thousand to one the signal about you will never have got through and even if it has the bloody Adjutant or some WAAF or other will have lost it. No, never be on time, old boy, never be on time.'

With such splendid subterfuges my friend was able constantly and easily to dodge all the more arduous or boring or irksome of duties. One of these consisted of an incredible afternoon when, herded into the camp cinema for an hour and a half, we were given a stunningly thrilling lecture on the social duties incumbent upon officers, in particular *The Art of the Social Afternoon Call on the Wives of Other Officers and the Leaving of Cards Therewith.*

When the three-week course was finally over I got the posting I expected: that of Flight-Lieutenant to Public Relations, Air Ministry. On the way out of camp my heavy cabin trunk was carelessly dropped from a truck, one of the sides bashed in. Instantly, properly inspired by the wisdom of my hotelier friend, I made it an excuse to snatch two days' leave at home. Nobody, as my friend had truly predicted, turned a hair.

II

When I eventually reported back to Air Ministry it was to find that the newly formed department of Public Relations, P.R.11, consisted of only four men, I now being the fifth: Hilary St George Saunders himself, an assistant Flight-Lieut., John Pudney and F. A. Walbank, who had produced one or two anthologies but, unlike John Pudney and myself, was not commissioned. In the various other departments of P.R. there were considerable numbers of other writers of much experience and distinction. Leonard Dodds and Dudley Barker were both later to become my chiefs and very excellent and understanding ones at that; many of the rest I never met at all and others not until some long time later. Among those I did meet, and indeed made good friends with, were Geoffrey Harmsworth, of the famous newspaper family, R. F. Delderfield, still a struggling playwright, with his phenomenally successful *Worm's Eye View* still to come, Eric Partridge, who had in fact published at his Scholartis Press a book of mine, *Seven Tales and Alexander*, Vernon Noble, Stanley Bishop, renowned as a crime reporter, John Macadam, sports writer, and Fletcher Allen, an editor. Also somewhere in the building were Alan Melville, John Strachey and Philip Guedalla, as well as artists and photographers of much distinction too.

John Pudney and I at once got on well together (indeed I can truthfully say that, with one single exception, I encountered nothing but friendliness in my entire RAF service). In sharp contrast to this was the behaviour of Hilary St George Saunders and his assistant Flight-Lieut. who daily and indeed almost all day engaged in prolonged and abusive slanging matches, carried out with a sort of rude verbal affection, love-hate, pitilessly, no holds barred. These encounters were a joy and wonder to behold and listen to. Hilary indeed was a master of fearless invective, a gift he used on not a few occasions in order to make easier the path of his newest pupil, to whom he now presently announced:

'We think we should send you first to a Bomber Station, where you can stay for two or three days in order to sense the atmosphere. The one we have in mind is at Oakington, just outside Cambridge. But first we'd like you to go to H.Q. Bomber Command at High Wycombe, where their head man will take you under his wing and see you on your way.'

There was little I could do but acquiesce in all this, though I did so with an increasing nervousness and apprehension. Once again I was assailed with the chilling fear that I might fail in my mission. Of bombers and bomber crews I knew nothing; the vocabulary and territory of that world, celestial or otherwise, were utterly foreign to me. Suppose it should happen that I boob, put up a black? Thankfully the understanding wisdom of John Nerney, that 'rock of integrity' as David Garnett has called him, was there to sustain me as I went to say good-bye to him before leaving for this, my first assignment. Somehow he managed to imply, without actually saying it, that all would be well, and my faith in myself was re-implanted.

Next day I was on my way to High Wycombe, in my car. I had scarcely cleared the suburbs of London before I was

flagged down by a Cockney gentleman seeking a lift. In true Cockney fashion he had the new, green Pilot Officer weighed up in about three minutes flat: the easy, dead easy touch. His trouble, he proceeded smoothly to explain, was that he'd been supposed to meet his brother that morning, in Ealing, but for some reason the brother hadn't turned up. They were in fact going to High Wycombe to pick up a set of car tyres and the brother, see, was the one who had the money. My Cockney passenger was now, of course, as he proceeded glibly to explain, in 'somefink of a spot'. He had three quid on him all right but he needed another five so as he could get the tyres. Did I know what? – if I could lend him the fiver he would later leave it at the *Poste Restante* at High Wycombe Post Office and I could call for it on my way back from wherever I was going to. See?

I fell. This, among the oldest of confidence tricks, was too much for, and completely mesmerised, my innocent good nature. I duly handed over the fiver and duly turned up, some days later, at High Wycombe Post Office, to emerge empty-handed. There is, however, a true and good saying, especially applicable, I think, to writers of fiction. It is to the effect that 'nothing is ever lost'. The incident of my Cockney friend and his confidence trick never left my mind, and more than twenty years later I turned it into a story, *Mr Featherstone Takes a Ride*, for which an editor paid me 250 guineas, thus showing a fair profit on a morning in which I too had been taken for one.

On arrival at H.Q. Bomber Command, High Wycombe, I was assailed by the illusion that I had, by some misguidance, strayed into the portals of the Ritz. All, it seemed to me, was grandeur. I had grown used to, in my three weeks' Officers' Training Course at Uxbridge, a certain prison-like shabbiness, even if sherry was only ninepence a glass. Here at High Wycombe the Mess Bar Steward was as impeccable as a first-class Head Waiter, dressed in a jacket as white as that of an umpire at Lord's. 'And what, sir, would you care to drink? We have everything. A little sherry perhaps? Bristol Milk? Bristol Cream? Thank you, sir. The Bristol Cream.'

After a lunch of an excellence only comparable with that of the Bristol Cream I drove on to Cambridge, guided and

accompanied by 'the head man'. It was, as I remember it,
a grey, damp and dismal November afternoon which grew
only greyer, damper and more dismal the farther north we got.
By the time we reached Cambridge it was almost dark; at
Oakington it was completely so, a circumstance that only
served to increase my already wavering fears and apprehen-
sions. Nor were these uplifted by the fact that at the RAF
station, in the Mess ante-room, a radio was belting out a
popular tune that has for ever remained in my mind as one of
haunting melancholy: *Daddy, let me stay up late*, which to this
day enshrines so much of the ephemeral nature of the lives
of the young bomber pilots and crews I was about to meet and
write about. It is not too much to say that I can never recall
that song, still less hear it, without being very near to tears.

But before I ever got to the Mess still another experience
deepened my gloom. It was my first sight of the giant Stirling
Bombers, lined up like so many black broody birds, apparently
either ready to roost for the night or to lay equally black and
destructive eggs, all round the perimeter of the airfield. Huge,
unwieldy, twenty-five feet or more high from ground to nose,
not easy to fly, desperately difficult to handle in a cross wind,

those monsters stood there in dark, sinister, ugly assembly. My one comforting thought, as I looked at them in the dimmed light of that November evening, was that I had been expressly forbidden, on Air Ministry instructions, thank God, to take any sort of part in Flying Operations. It was no small expression of Air Ministry's Public Relations wisdom that my job was to write stories and not, by the Grace of God, to get myself unnecessarily killed.

When at last I found myself in the Mess ante-room it was to be further assailed by the impression that I had somehow strayed into a gathering of Sixth Form schoolboys grown prematurely old. I think it true to say that of all the officers assembled there that evening scarcely more than a dozen were over twenty-five. One of these was the Station Commander, Group-Captain Adams, an extraordinarily likeable and able man who looked rather more like a sea captain from Drake's time than an R.A.F. officer; another was an American from Texas, known naturally as Tex, a rear-gunner of small stature but extremely powerful hands who had got himself into the R.A.F. in order to wage a purely personal war against Hitler; another was a Kentish man, Norman Winch, who had done some journalism but was really hoping to be a farmer and who, I am happy to say, is now a farmer and has been my good friend, together with his pretty wife, ever since; another was myself, so ancient at 36 that it would not have at all surprised me if the young pilots had called me Pop.

It was the eyes of these young but prematurely aged officers that made a first powerful and everlasting impact on me. They were not 'sicklied o'er with the pale cast of thought' or even that of fear. It was something much more elusive, profound, disturbing and hard to define. Perhaps I can best illustrate it by telling of a young Australian pilot of whom, eventually, I was to write two or three stories. He had come from a family of sheep-farmers, up country, in Victoria: lean, indeed gaunt of face, tight of lip, eyes glassy and seemingly sightless, almost, from long night fatigue. I grew very attached to him before he was finally shot down and killed over Germany.

15

When his parents and his sister at last read the stories that I wrote of him they had one paramount desire: to come to meet the man who had written of the son and brother they had lost. The war eventually being over, they came to see me: simple, honest, proud, rural people steeped in pride for a young man who had given his life 12,000 miles from home. With such pride as parents naturally have on these occasions they showed me a photograph of him taken when he had first joined the Royal Australian Air Force: a mere boy, starry-eyed, proud too, the new entrant on his way to the big school.

I weep as I write these words: I did not recognise him. Nor, as I handed them my own photograph of him, the gaunt-faced, glassy-eyed, weary veteran of Heaven knew what Hell had been his lot over Germany, did they recognise him either. In silence, they far more shocked than I, we realised that we were speaking of two different men.

Such was my initiation into the world of Bomber Command; and that night, as I went to bed, I knew that Air Ministry's suggested 'two or three days' would have at least to be two or three weeks, perhaps even two or three months. The immediate problem was to get these men to talk; but how? That was the question. I knew of course of that great unwritten R.A.F. law: the one that forbids the shooting of lines. But somehow lines had to be shot or extracted: whether in secret, by trickery, subterfuge or even some form of cheating I didn't yet know.

Next morning I met the Wing Commander of No. 7 Squadron, a tough young man who viewed with a certain suspicion, if not indeed resentment, the writer from Air Ministry. Nevertheless we talked; and as we talked I solved the first of my problems: I would play the game of eavesdropping. Accordingly, that morning, I got my first story, unwittingly given to me by the unsuspecting Wing Commander who, in an unguarded moment, let fall some remark to the effect that the worst of his own problems was that of writing to relatives of men killed or even of seeing them in his office as they turned up, pitifully hoping, perhaps, that by some sort of miracle he would conjure their beloved ones back from the dead. 'It's Hell,' he said, 'but then that's just the way it is.'

This, in fact, was what I called the story, *It's Just the Way It Is*, and this is how it began:

November rain falls harshly on the clean tarmac, and the wind, turning suddenly, lifts sprays of yellow elm leaves over the black hangars.

This clear, pictorial simplicity was, I felt, the right and only way that this story, and indeed any others, should be written. I wrote it the following day, in a couple of hours, and posted it straight off to Hilary Saunders, half-dreading what he might have to say about it. In no time there came back from Whitehall a stream of delighted cries and I was able to breathe again.

My next task was to make friends; and this I did, drinking with pilots and navigators, playing cribbage with them, exchanging purposely idle gossip, hardly ever mentioning ops, bombers or writing. Soon a certain air of tension that my arrival had built up began to be dissipated. In a week my presence was accepted, warmly, often with much humour, and without suspicion.

Almost the first thing I had noted about these bomber crews, and which never afterwards failed to fascinate me, was their international democracy. Canadians, Scots, Australians, Rhodesians, Tex the American, Englishmen, Irishmen, Welshmen, New Zealanders: the mixture of nationalities was great. Perhaps an even more striking thing was that of rank. It not infrequently happened that one of those great Stirlings would be piloted and captained by a sergeant, who might have under his command men of the rank of pilot-officer or flight-lieutenant. Rank in fact became meaningless as crews set out for the blackness over Germany. Many of these sergeants, in fact, neither wanted nor sought commissions. They preferred the *camaraderie* of the sergeants' mess, well knowing that a sergeant, as pilot and captain, could expect and receive utter obedience and respect from men superior, however superior, to him in rank. And this, it seemed to me, was a wonderful thing.

Beer was the main drink of these flying men and off duty they swilled at it pretty heavily. It is not a drink I greatly care for but I confess to having drunk more of it in my three months at Oakington (for three months was it to become) than either before or since. Fortunately there were more refined sources of refreshment and one of these was the Arts Theatre Restaurant in Cambridge, where the excellent cellar had been built up by wines given from various college cellars. And it was here that I presently began to take a pilot, perhaps two, to dinner so that we could talk, over a bottle of wine, far out of range of Mess ears. Again I played the game of eavesdropping, never pumping my guests for stories, content always to pick up the creative crumbs as they fell.

They fell pretty frequently and I, like an artist catching a quick glimpse of a face, a scene, a horse, a bird on the wing, made from them my quick-sketched stories, using always the simple, clear graphic approach. Almost always, I think, these flying companions utterly failed to realize that it was the casual, unsuspecting, apparently irrelevant word that I was waiting for as my inspiration. I will give two instances. One evening a pilot, an extraordinarily good and tough one, let fall the casual statement that sometimes, not returning from ops over Germany until dawn was breaking, he would see the sun rise twice, once from several thousand feet up and a second time after he had landed. I could scarcely wait to get this illuminating symbolic episode down on paper and when I did so I called it *The Sun Rises Twice*.

The second incident fell from the lips of the young Australian of whom I have already spoken, Geoff Heard, and it almost drove me wild with excitement. There had been, it seemed, on a remote sheep-farm in Victoria, a couple with an only son. So precious and useful were his hands in the running of the sheep-farm that when war broke out the parents instantly resorted to every kind of trick and subterfuge in order to keep the news from him. Newspapers were cancelled, letters were opened, hidden or burnt, the radio was put out of action. All this, combined with the extreme remoteness of the station, enabled them to keep the stark fact of war from him for an entire year. Then, inevitably, there came a day when he drove a hundred miles to the nearest good-sized town for a few days' holiday, went into a barber's saloon for a haircut, picked up a newspaper and was stunned by the greatest shock of his young life. He enlisted the very next day and I called his story *The Young Man from Kalgoorlie.*

Cambridge, besides the sheer everlasting beauty of its colleges, had other civilised pleasures to offer. Two or three times a week there were afternoon orchestral concerts and to these I often went with some fellow officers not on duty, to listen to Mozart, Bach, Schubert and others. One of these officers was a small, shy, soft-spoken young Irishman who behaved and looked more like a gentle poet than a fighting man. I admired and liked him so much that I truly believe that if he had asked me to go on ops with him I would have flouted Air Ministry rules and have gone with him. Fortunately he made no such suggestion; and after lunch one day I stood on the perimeter of the airfield and watched his big Stirling take off for Brest, there to attack the two German battleships *Scharnhorst* and *Gneisenau* popularly known as Salmon and Gluckstein. The plane had scarcely risen to five hundred feet or so when it suddenly seemed to blossom into a great orange and crimson flower. It fell in fields, wreathed in a vast black pall of smoke, a mile or two away.

It was Canadians, mostly, who provided a physical toughness far removed from the poetic gentleness of my young Irish friend. One of these, a hefty navigator named Mac, was for ever, in true Canadian fashion, spoiling for a fight. We not infrequently went out together, often with another Canadian, Ed Baker, and Norman Winch, and sometimes with an extremely pretty blonde WAAF officer named Christine to whom we were all rather attached. One evening as we sat over drinks in a hotel bar I was amazed to see the two Canadians suddenly rise swiftly to their feet, simply seize a man on the other side of the room, frog-march him through the door and hurl him with unceremonial violence into the street. The reason?

'The guy was undressing Christine with his eyes.'

But even this brief episode of violence was as nothing compared with another memorable encounter that, a few nights later, Mac enjoyed in London, where he had gone on leave. When he finally returned to Oakington his appearance was like that of a man who had been in a fifteen round contest with Jack Dempsey, Joe Louis and Rocky Marciano all at the same time. His face was a red-and-purple mass of bruises and lacerations; his eyes were mere swollen red bags; his tunic was torn and stiff with dark, dried blood.

When I inquired as to the reason for this disturbing sight Mac informed me with calmness that it was nothing. Just nothing. Nothing. Just a fight.

'Some fight.'

'No. Just an ordinary fight.'

Mac, it seemed, had gone into the men's room at the Regent Palace Hotel, there to find three big men picking on a little one. Such an excuse for a scrap was on no account to be missed and Mac merrily mowed in.

'And how did it finally turn out?' I wanted to know.

'Oh! they took 'em away in ambulances.'

Looking at the lacerated face of my Canadian friend I could only marvel and wonder, trying to guess the state of his defeated adversaries. Ordinary fight indeed.

Not very long later Mac was on ops over Italy, where he was shot down, wounded and taken prisoner-of-war. In typical fashion, after a few days in hospital, he mesmerised a young Italian nurse into letting him have slightly more than the regulation amount of freedom and thus instantly escaped and, having escaped, promptly proceeded to walk to Rome, where he knocked on the door of the Vatican.

There he was given a suit of civilian clothes, a seat on a plane and a day later was back in England.

At lunch one day, trying to force down my throat a dreary plateful of bully beef and potatoes (the food at Oakington was on the whole sadly uninspired) I was called to the telephone. At the other end of the line was Hilary Saunders, informing me that I had been summoned to the immediate presence of no less a person than the Secretary of State for Air.

When I finally reached Whitehall, filled with a certain apprehension at my summons there, and was shown into the ministerial presence, it was to find Sir Archibald Sinclair, a man of highly distinguished appearance, indeed aristocratic of presence without being aloof, and of great personal charm and impeccable politeness. His American mother and Winston Churchill's American mother were cousins. I consequently felt no little honoured that he had not only greatly admired my stories but had sent for me personally in order to offer his congratulations. It gave me satisfaction to feel that, in spite of all my doubts and forebodings, I had gone some way towards justifying the faith that Hilary Saunders, Harald Peake and John Nerney (and also David Garnett, the original moving spirit behind it all) had had in me. At the same time I was told that the stories were soon to be published and that Hilary had been inspired to invent for me the pseudonym *Flying Officer X*.

The stories duly appeared in *The News Chronicle* under that *nom de plume*, which in fact hid my identity for just about a single day. My imprint, it seemed, was on every word. When I got back to Oakington the first of the *News Chronicle* stories had already been widely read and I felt a sense of inexplicable unease. There was much leg-pulling; and the Wing Commander, I was told, was gunning for me. The Station Commander was fortunately far more tolerant but even so I took the first opportunity of making some excuse to go back to Air Ministry, with the avowed intention of begging Hilary to give me a few days' leave, which in his typically generous fashion he did. Later it was of no little satisfaction to me to know that the men of Bomber Command themselves approved of the stories; it seemed that the right, authentic, unheroic note had been struck; the stories were also much read, I understand, in prisoner-of-war camps and today, I am assured, still offer much interest to a generation unacquainted with either Bomber Command or the war.

When I again got back to Oakington the air was calmer, my unease had disappeared and I even found myself being congratulated by the WAAF telephone operator who had all unwittingly provided me, sometimes, with material for stories too, often in circumstances painful to her, when she had to inform me that she was afraid 'Flight-Lieut. so-and-so had bought it, over Bremen last night'. She was a girl of much quiet charm and I fear there were often tears in her eyes.

But now a momentous event occurred. The chief Station Intelligence Officer, an agreeable man who had done much to make my early passage smooth, one day suggested that I go and have a talk with him. He had, he felt, something to tell me that might be of considerable interest. We duly talked, I being sworn to secrecy. It appeared that the Captain of a Wellington Bomber shot down over France had escaped by devious routes and was now back with his Squadron, which though not specifically stationed at Oakington, nevertheless shared our Mess; and it seemed that he had a remarkable story to tell.

The point about secrecy arose from the fact that in those comparatively early days any mention in public of pilots escaping after being shot down over the Continent was strictly taboo. But, the Intelligence Officer informed me, I could if I wished talk to the pilot, though only on the absolute condition that I neither breathed nor wrote a word of what he had to tell. Next day I met and talked with the pilot and the seed of *Fair Stood the Wind For France* was sown.

Partly because of the immediate excitement of this, partly because so many of the men I had first known in No. 7 Squadron had now either been killed or taken prisoner (there were some deeply dark days on that often fog-shrouded fen-land that winter) I felt it a propitious moment in which to leave Oakington and seek new stories elsewhere. I also felt that, regardless of all rules and swearing to secrecy, the Wellington Bomber pilot's story must, somehow, be got down on paper. I therefore resolved to tell Hilary that I needed a change of scene and a break before we could decide on the exploration of 'fresh woods and pastures new'. Hilary, ever understanding and in any case pleased that he had put his money, by some good chance, on a horse that wasn't quite an also-ran, duly gave me leave and I went home, my brain and imagination positively bursting like a ripe seed-pod under the heat and fervour of the story I wanted to tell.

I wrote as in a fever, the words nevertheless cool, simple, graphic, restrained. The seed given me by the Wellington pilot was seed only; it now had to be sown and nurtured in the soil of imagination, as of course all fiction has to be. I had first to invent the bomber crew; then their disastrous moment of being shot down; then their being hidden and aided by a French family, among whom the young daughter was of supreme, proud and electric importance. Indeed I saw the entire story as one epitomising the youth of two countries, on the one hand England almost alone in battle, on the other France alone in humiliation and defeat. I wanted to extract from this, if possible, the beauty, the pride, the courage and, if the word is not now too suspect, the patriotism of the young of two civilised countries determined that they would in no circumstances be slaves to an oppressor. If there was also an air of fatalism about it all so it had to be; it was just the way it was.

Dates and times are now a little difficult to recall with accuracy, but I think I had a fortnight's leave, in which I wrote, I can only suppose, very nearly half the novel. One more thing I had to invent was that particular part of the French countryside in which the events, especially the escape of the pilot, had to be set. The northern part of France I already knew; but south of Paris I had never been. Nor, of course, had I ever been to the city of Marseilles, where the final scenes of the novel were to be enacted. All this too had to be conjured from imagination, but at the same time with topographical accuracy and, in the case of Marseilles, with some sort of urban accuracy. I duly read my maps, my guides

23

to France and my Baedekers. I like to think, now, that I got most of these things right, though eventually Hilary, who knew France far better than I did, informed me that I had caused sugar-beet to be grown in a part of France where, in fact, it never was.

So, at week-ends, in odd moments, in a few days of leave, I wrote *Fair Stood the Wind For France*, taking the title from the immortal words of Michael Drayton, Shakespeare's contemporary who, in fact, wrote at least one sonnet comparable in quality with those of the great man himself: *Since there's no help, come let us kiss and part*. He also wrote, in the poem beginning *Fair Stood the Wind For France*, the perfect plan for the prevention of the D-Day invasion of France by Allied Troops, a plan fortunately ignored by the stupid Hitler and his advisers and generals:

> *'But putting to the main*
> *At Caux, the mouth of Seine,*
> *With all his martial train*
> *Landed King Harry.'*

So indeed we did land; it was by no means the first time that Englishmen had landed at that particular point in France or, in fact, defeated their enemies there.

In this way I left Oakington and the grey, fog-bound and so often dismal fen-lands. The countryside, except for the colleges of Cambridge and the superb cathedral at Ely, had not inspired me; the men of No. 7 Squadron and their ugly, difficult bombers had.

It was now decided that I should go to No. 1 Fighter Command Station at Tangmere, just outside Chichester, midway between the luscious Sussex Downs above Cowdray Park and the sea. The weather was bitterly cold and the atmosphere in the Mess, alas, hardly less so. I wandered about for days in a state of lonely misery, scarcely speaking to a soul. There was, it seemed to me, in contrast to the warmth of Oakington, a certain chill snobbery in the air. I once tried an approach to an Australian, who merely turned on me a cool

deaf ear. I tried chatting to New Zealanders and felt myself to be in the presence of aloof, petty provincials. My one and only contact with a South African merely revealed the presence of a Boer who was a boor. I was uneasy in the company of the Station Commander, who viewed my invasion of his hitherto jealously guarded kingdom with a certain high suspicion. Nowhere could I detect a keyhole, still less a key, that would grant me entrance into a world containing stories. I felt near to despair. In addition to all this there was no bed for me in the base and I was put into an otherwise empty house some distance away and there slept and brooded alone.

I developed a strong suspicion that this lack of co-operation stemmed from the Station Commander himself. I accordingly went back to Air Ministry, there to speak with Hilary about it. Hilary was vexed and firm. 'You are beholden to no one but Air Ministry and if your precious Station Commander fails to co-operate we shall deal with him appropriately.' After that I went back to Tangmere with spirits slightly lifted and then, by a piece of good fortune, things improved.

One day in the Mess I noticed a young Squadron-Leader, standing well over six feet, whom I hadn't seen before. He had

no left hand. In its place he had been fitted with a metal gadget which looked rather like a complicated egg-whisk. Perhaps the shattering experience of losing his hand combined with a fanatical determination to go on flying, in spite of it, had given him more humanity than some of his fellows. At all events we talked; his name was McLauchlan; and presently he was inviting me to meet some of the pilots of the renowned No. 1 Squadron, of which he was leader. No. 1 Squadron was by now a night fighter squadron and perhaps it was the experience of flying by night that gave its pilots some of the warmth and kinship that I had so much liked and admired at Oakington. At last, I felt, I had my keyhole and my key.

One of these pilots was a Czech named Kuttelwacher. He too had had a shattering experience: namely that of escaping from his native country by the most devious and adventurous of routes through Southern Europe, Turkey, the Mediterranean and Heaven knew where. He was a man of much humour and gaiety and McLauchlan had dreamed up the idea of shooting up trains and airfields in France at night, operations the two of them carried out with joyous rivalry and glee. I too felt joyous, seizing on these events like a hungry dog long deprived of bones; and this is how, at the time, I described it all:

'It was one of those periods in a station when the unity and life of a good Squadron becomes too strong to remain a local thing, compressed within itself, meaning something to only a few people. It breaks out, and spreading, warm and energetic and fluid, becomes a large thing, meaning something to many people.

'It was one of those periods when everything was good. The weather was good and calm and sunny, the sea-light lofty and pure over the sea by day. The nights were good and starry, with no ground mist and just the right cover of cloud. The Squadron was good and proud and knew itself. The things it did were good and the news of its doings was in the papers. Whenever you came into the Mess or the billiard-room or the dining-room and heard laughter boiling over too richly you knew it was that Squadron laughing. You knew by their laughter that they wanted nothing else than to be kept as they were, flying by night together, shooting up trains on the flat lands of Northern France, shooting down careless Dorniers over their own aerodrome. They had found each other. The positive and exuberant feeling of their discovery spread over the Station, from Erks to Waafs and from Waafs to officers, until all of us felt it there.'

By this time, too, winter had broken, letting in spring at last to the luscious Sussex hills, to which I used to repair with another kind of hunger, famished for the sight of bluebells and primroses, may-blossom and oaks in green-gold flower. To roam those hills was an experience of heart-breaking beauty, infinitely precious. Our bodily hunger was also well taken care of at Tangmere. The Mess Fund was rich, carrying an enormous surplus by means of which the Mess Secretary was able to fill us with out-of-season delights. On my arrival he had even apologised for the fact that dinner in the evening had unfortunately to be cut down from seven courses to a mere five, a difference that after Oakington's sparse fare did not in the least depress me.

Unhappily there came a day when, going back to Air Ministry, I found Hilary Saunders no longer there. He had been transferred to Combined Operations. Worse still, P.R.11 had been disbanded and I found myself in a new department, P.R.3, among new faces. In Hilary's place, however, was an extremely agreeable officer, Leonard Dodds, with Fletcher Allen as a sort of second-in-command. On my very first afternoon at P.R.3 I gave Fletcher, affectionately known as Fletch, a not inconsiderable shock.

At half past three I was preparing to leave the office when Fletch stopped me.

'And where, Bates, may I ask, do you think you are going?'

'Home.'

'*You are going where?*'

'Home.'

'Good God. May I inform you that no one leaves this office until seven o'clock?'

'You may inform me but I am nevertheless still going home.'

'Good God, are you out of your mind? Are you due for leave or something?'

'No.'

'Then what the hell are you going home for?'

'I am going home to write.'

'Very interesting. *Most* interesting. Is it too much to ask, perhaps, that you write here? Couldn't you, perhaps, do that?'

'No. Not the sort of writing I want to do.'

'And what, may I ask, is the sort of writing you want to do?'

'A story.'

'And how long, if it is not too much to ask, will you be away?'

'A week. Very probably two. You see, it's a very long story. And I think a very important one.'

Thereafter Fletch was speechless but, being also human, he relented and let me go. A couple of weeks later I came back

28

with the longest *Flying Officer X* story I had yet written, *How Sleep the Brave*, and Fletch, having read it at one gulp, went into raptures of excitement. So P.R.3 accepted me on the terms Hilary had long since promised. I was a free agent, moving and writing where, how and when I liked.

Some time before Hilary had left Air Ministry he had put his own enthusiasm for the *Flying Officer X* stories into the practical proposition that they should be published in book form. I felt much honoured by this but rather less pleased when he told me that he thought the firm of Macmillan should be the publishers. I said that, on the contrary, since Jonathan Cape had been my publishers for sixteen years, they should be offered the book instead. Hilary at once agreed and immediately picked up the telephone to talk to Cape. I then remembered that Jonathan Cape himself was ill and said that Hilary should talk instead to Wren Howard, his partner.

'Right,' he said. 'And why not listen on the extension?

Hilary and Wren Howard duly talked and I listened. The attitude of Wren Howard, at first, could only be likened to a hard frost. There were long periods of silence, clearly denoting a strong air of suspicion touched with an equally strong lack of enthusiasm. Then Hilary played, quite casually, a trump card.

'You would, of course, be given all the paper you need. Unlimited paper.'

Paper being, at that period of the war, as precious as platinum, the change of atmosphere at the other end of the telephone was instant and miraculous.

'What we have in mind,' Hilary then said, 'is that our edition should be a sort of Penguin, selling at sixpence, but that you may do your own hard-back edition at, perhaps, half-a-crown.'

The temperature at the other end of the telephone rose as in a heat-wave.

The ultimate results of this conversation I shall describe in more detail later.

Meanwhile there came a day when Group-Captain Dodds,

affectionately known to us all as Doddie, as indeed he still is today, sent for me one morning and said:

'Old boy, they are going to publish your *Flying Officer X* stories any moment now. And guess what?'

I had nothing I could possibly guess.

'First printing will be 100,000.'

Never having heard of a book, except the Bible and *Gone with the Wind*, selling such figures, I nearly fainted.

III

In periods of leave, at week-ends or whenever I could snatch a spare day I now worked on *Fair Stood the Wind For France*, writing in a frenzy that fitted the mood of the times yet always striving to keep the style of the novel, as in the stories of *Flying Officer X*, clear and vivid in its pictorial simplicity. What exactly would happen to the book if and when it was finished I was as yet unable to tell. It might have been that if I had shown it to Authority I could well have incurred much displeasure since I had flouted regulations on security about escapes, which were still very strict. It might also have been that even if I incurred no such displeasure or reprimand the appropriate department in charge of security might not have been given the necessary clearance for publication. A third possibility was that Air Ministry might well have said that, since the book had been written in service time and from material provided by another serving officer, they would claim the book as theirs, leaving me without a penny profit; and Heaven knew that I needed every penny I could get.

Fortunately there now began to be slight signs that security regulations relating to escapes were relaxing; and soon, as they still further relaxed, I decided to show the now finished novel to Fletcher Allen. Ever since I had written *How Sleep the Brave* Fletch had shown an increasing tendency to regard me as his own *protégé*, covering me with an increasingly protective wing. I therefore thought I could rely on his discretion.

When Fletch had finished the novel he instantly jumped into a new ecstasy of admiration and excitement. Not only was the book marvellously good, he declared, but come Hell or high water it was going to remain my own. The business of clearance ought not, he thought, to be difficult, after which he declared with every ounce of conviction that the book

31

would be a best-seller. The pleasure at hearing this was presently slightly tempered by a mild reprimand. To Fletch's infinite astonishment he discovered that I had not, and never had had, an agent to handle my affairs. Such folly was unthinkable and had at once to be rectified. 'I will arrange at once that you meet my friend Laurence Pollinger.'

So, for the first time, I met the man who has handled my increasingly complicated affairs ever since. We instantly got on extremely well together and it can truthfully be said that that first meeting, like that with Edward Garnett, was dramatically to change the course of my life. Among other things it also led to my changing, after some seventeen years, my publisher.

Laurence Pollinger has ever been a tireless and watchful champion in the battle for the protection of authors' rights and the rectification of the injustices that are often done to them. He had, of course, heard of the wide success happily attained by the *Flying Officer X* stories and he now inquired how well, financially, I had done with them. When I replied that I had of course received not a penny other than my officer's pay he was both astounded and angry. But what, he inquired, about Cape? Had Cape not slipped a guinea or two into my hand? A box of chocolates into my wife's? They had not, I declared, nor had they slipped a drink, a lunch, a case of wine; indeed they had made no material gesture of thanks whatever, though they had sold countless thousands of copies of *The Greatest People in the World* and *How Sleep the Brave*.

This further fanned the flames of Laurence's anger. 'Do you then propose,' he asked, 'to let them publish *Fair Stood the Wind For France?*' I replied that I had firmly and irrevocably decided not to. This pleased him. And to whom, he asked, did I think of taking the book? He had only to show it to any one of twenty publishers and he was sure they would, like Fletcher Allen, jump for joy. Without hesitation my mind went back to my first meeting, nearly ten years before, with

Michael Joseph. M.J., I declared, was to be my man.

Instantly there was set up, at No. 30 Bedford Square, the house of Cape, a strong resistance movement. Was I not aware that my last contract, in its final clause, gave them the option on my next two books? I said that I was well aware, but it so happens that such a clause has no validity in law. It is what is termed 'a contract to make a contract' and is not, I fear, worth the paper it is written on. So came my parting with Cape and not, I think, without good cause.

Michael Joseph, at this time, wasn't enjoying the best of health (my own, at the same time, was deteriorating rapidly, the old abdominal pains getting more and more severe, leaving me all too often grey of spirit, sleepless at night and haggard with exhaustion) and the man in charge at No. 26 Bloomsbury Street was Robert, now Sir Robert, Lusty. Bob treated me with sense and generosity, giving me a fat, unbelievably fat, advance on the book. As Laurence Pollinger was also able to sell the serial rights of it to both England and America and negotiate yet another excellent advance from *The Atlantic Monthly* I found myself, almost for the first time in my life, free of financial anxiety.

After twenty years of writing, with its several disasters and constant struggles, *Fair Stood the Wind For France* was my first wide success. The book was translated into many languages, and indeed is still being further translated, and at least one perceptive reviewer saw it, as I had intended it to be, a story epitomising the youth of two countries at a period of great conflict and agony. Part of the story concerns the amputation, in great and dangerous secrecy, by a French doctor, of an English R.A.F. pilot's arm, and I hope I shall not appear guilty of self-praise if I say that, many and many a time, not only in England but abroad, I met admirers of the book who took one look of astonishment at me and marvelled that I still possessed *both* of my arms. This is, or should be, a verification of Thackeray's dictum that 'the work of fiction contains more truth in solution than the work which purports to be all true.' It is indeed true to say that there were times when I was writing the description of that amputation I really felt that it was, in fact, my own arm that was being cut off.

By this time the war had reached a strange, tense, darkening phase. In some ways it was rather like being trapped in a powerless train in a long, black suffocating tunnel. One felt gripped by a ghastly inertia, a ghoulish nightmare in which the end of the tunnel could not only not be seen but seemed as if it would never, never be there. There appeared to be neither daylight nor hope. Destruction of shipping by U-Boats piled up to a scale excruciating, savage, vastly perilous. There used to be a pair of lady comics, Gert and Daisy, who sang songs of cheer on the radio, interspersing them with remarks such as 'We go to bed hopeful and wake up thankful'. To this day I wonder how, at times, we had the heart to continue with either hope or thanks.

Yet, all this time, more and more people were returning to the capital. The vortex of the whole grim unease was there, in London's heart, and one felt that one had to be part of its agony. Now and then I returned to Tangmere or to other Stations, hoping, as a man mushrooming or birds' nesting on a summer's day, to find a scrap of treasure that would translate itself into a story. It rarely happened. A sortie or two over the French coast, an enemy fighter shot down, one of our own pilots lost: of great drama, as in the Battle of Britain, there was little or none. On occasions pilots went out over the Channel to have a 'look-see' and either saw little or, as in the case of the Station Commander of Tangmere one fine summer afternoon, got themselves killed. An era of apparent pointlessness, of pacific or half-pacific pause, seemed to have arrived. Where were we going, if anywhere? I used to ask myself. Why the hell, indeed, were we doing it at all?

Somewhere about this time, to my great dismay, Group-Captain Leonard Dodds was posted to India. He had been a wholly understanding chief, urbane of humour, understanding in matters such as giving complete freedom of movement to a writer of imagination, never once confusing a uniform with

34

a strait jacket. We had got on supremely well together and I knew that I should miss him greatly. My fear was, I think, that some narrow-gutted tyrant, a petty king, might take his place.

Happily it was not so. Doddie was presently succeeded by Group-Captain Dudley Barker, an experienced and very able journalist who also, very fortunately, understood that writers of imaginative ability cannot be regimented even if and when you put them into uniform. Dudley and I also got on, I am glad to say, supremely well together and it was to him, some time later, that I was to owe a great debt. He, like Edward Garnett and others before him, was to accomplish yet another revolution in my life: of which I shall have much more to say later.

One day I received a summons to Dudley Barker's desk, there to be told that no less a person than Air-Chief Marshal Portal (later Lord Portal) wished to see me: in fact not only to see me but to take me out to lunch. I had instant visions of having committed some appalling misdemeanour, which in turn would involve demotion (by now I was a Squadron-Leader), severe reprimand or a dismissal to some arid diabolical post, such as Aden, far from my beloved England. Happily, again, it was not so.

The meeting with Portal proved not only to be pleasant; it confirmed once again, in my experience at any rate, that the higher one got in the realms of Service Rank, the more impressive were, with very few exceptions, its members. I had already been much impressed by Sir Archibald Sinclair; I had been equally impressed by Lord Willoughby de Broke, who had always shown me, even in my modest rank of Pilot Officer, all courtesy, understanding and friendliness. ('Hullo, Bates. Sit down. Take a pew, old boy. What now? Splendid stories of yours, dear fellow. What can I do to help?') It was only when one met people of the middle orders – what in Northamptonshire language we should call piss-quicks – that there was aroused in one a disquieting sense of inferiority. The aristocracy did not, I found, wave their flags of superiority.

35

The middle and lower orders, I fear, very often did. For this reason their few members shall be nameless.

I do not now recall where Portal took me to lunch but it was most probably, I think, his club. If I had any lingering disturbances of thought as we met they were soon dispersed. I found myself in the presence of a man of intelligence, charm, good conversation and width of vision. I think I am right in saying that we had reached the stage of the coffee before he disclosed exactly the reason why he had singled me out from the company of my fellow Public Relations officers for some specialised purpose; and when it came I was slightly surprised. It was his idea, he proceeded to explain, that someone should write the story of the Night Battle of Britain, a perilous affair whose near-catastrophic events had already been allowed to slip back into a darkness as Stygian as that in which it had in fact been fought in the winter of 1941. Whereas the Battle of Britain had been blown up by infinite publicity into a sort of *Boy's Own Paper* adventure serial (and I am not attempting by one iota to detract from its formidable and high significance as a battle, comparable as it is with Trafalgar, with which it alone shares a day specifically named after it in the British calendar) the Night Battle had somehow slid away into the limbo of nightmares apparently best forgotten.

It was Portal's idea that this state of affairs should be put right. He proceeded to elaborate by comparing the two battles: the day battle an affair largely waged by one force, one section of the populace so small that its members had already been honoured as the Few; the night battle waged by comparison with scores of varied units drawn from all sections of the community, both service and civilian, as I have already described in *The Blossoming World*.

How we survived these deficiencies and their attendant and bloody ordeal, as I have also remarked in *The Blossoming World*, it is impossible to tell. Small wonder that Coventry was soon a blackened heap of masonry, its Cathedral a burnt-out skeleton, that London burned like tinder, its underground stations packed with thousands of refugees hoping and hoping

36

for a bloodless morning, or that the ancient and beautiful cities of Canterbury, Exeter and Bristol had the flower of their long heritage destroyed. The great and eternal wonder is that it wasn't a thousand times worse. But, as the subsequent history of aerial warfare in various parts of the world has proved, the dropping of vast quantities of wickedly explosive material on civilian populations, of whatever colour, class or creed, may kill but does not necessarily and finally destroy. In precisely the same way as Jewry has resisted and even flourished under centuries of persecution (in Britain it is at present in decline precisely because it is *not* persecuted) so a populace scourged and persecuted by bombs may emerge from the ordeal fewer in numbers but greater in resistance and strength, determined in spite of all odds not to be crushed. Whether you call this a triumph of mind over matter, of dignity over savagery, of civilisation over the jungle, it is exactly what happened to Britain in the Night Battle of Britain in 1941. We emerged bloody but unbowed.

The pamphlet was duly finished but, though approved in high places, was never published. Today it is safely filed away in the Public Records Office, from which it will doubtless never emerge. After I had finished it the war entered, as far as I was concerned, a new phase of inertia. Nor was this alleviated by my health, which continued to deteriorate, so much so that I endured almost constant abdominal pain, was unable to sleep at night and eventually was driven to beg Leonard Dodds, before his departure for India, to give me leave to go home and see my own doctor. This cry of despair followed innumerable visits to R.A.F. doctors who, after all the usual routine checks, one by one pronounced me A1, Grade 1. Never was a verdict on man's health a greater travesty.

In due course I found myself in hospital, attended by an embarrassing number of nurses and swallowing a revolting concoction known as a Barium meal, in preparation for an X-ray. This having been done I requested to be given the plate in order to report back to Group-Captain Dodds with proof that I had in fact been under hospital scrutiny. Not the least part of Doddie's endearing qualities is a certain wry sense of humour and when I duly reported back to him with the X-ray plate of my stomach, which incidentally revealed something known as a *duodenal diverticulum* he immediately sent it to the photographic department of P.R., which then spent the better part of an afternoon trying to elucidate from it which part of Berlin had been bombed the previous night. My own doctor's verdict sounded a rather more ominous note: 'One day we shall have to take a little peep inside you.'

All this, combined with the fact that I now had few if any stories to write, made me feel that the war had come to a premature dead end. It hadn't of course; but the plain fact was that the writing of pamphlets and articles was dull stuff compared with the stimulating, gay and often tragic days at Oakington, when I had been at the vortex of a whirl of action and comradeship the impact of which I knew would never fade. I longed for some opportunity, such as another *Fair Stood the Wind For France*, to use my imagination, but none was to come for another year or two. Meanwhile I did my best with bread-and-butter jobs and once even wrote a parliamentary speech for Sir Archibald Sinclair which he duly praised and delivered in the Commons.

This is not to say that our galleried room at P.R. was dull; very far from it. My friend and colleague R. F. Delderfield has well described it as a sort of Writers' Club, where rank counted for nothing and an atmosphere of great friendliness prevailed. Nevertheless I felt considerably frustrated, a situation in which I was certainly not alone. For what we were all waiting for at that time, I suppose, was the invasion of Hitler's Europe and there were times when the prospect of that event seemed a thousand years away.

Eventually, however, it began to build up to its inevitable climax. The air began to be full of rumours; the woods of the south country were filled with camouflaged guns and tanks. Soon, together with the rest of my colleagues at P.R., I was being given my assignment for D-Day. To my great joy I was to go back to Tangmere, there to cover, in a series of despatches designed specifically for American eyes, the first fighter assaults across the Channel. The actual date of the invasion still being a closely guarded secret, I again went through a period of much frustration, idly kicking my heels between Air Ministry and home, until eventually the tension of waiting grew unbearable and I at last took the road to Tangmere.

When I arrived there on a warm June afternoon I found every inch of space occupied by fighter squadrons, many of whom were aggressive, seething Canadians, raring for battle. There was not a bed to be had. Accordingly, after receiving the inevitable hypodermic jabs for this, that and the other, I drove into Chichester and got myself a room at the Dolphin Hotel, then suddenly started to feel uncommonly ill and repaired immediately to bed. There, remembering my friend the hotelier's consistent injunction never to be on time anywhere, I resolved to sleep late the following day. It was in fact a mere half past nine when I woke, feeling much better, and went placidly downstairs to what I hoped would be a leisurely breakfast. Sitting waiting for it I was, however, horrified to hear two ladies at the next table loudly discussing the fact that invasion had begun. I instantly swallowed a cup of tea, dashed out of the hotel to my car and drove at breakneck speed to Tangmere, cursing myself all the way for being fool enough to chance my luck once too often and considerably scared of the wrath of Air Ministry to come for my having failed in my assignment.

I needn't have worried; if invasion had indeed begun there was little sign of it at Tangmere. It is true that several squadrons had taken to the air but none were yet back from the scene of the battle they had so long thirsted for. It must have been eleven o'clock before the first of them began to appear from over the sea, their gay red-and-white candy striped wings brilliant against a deceptively hot blue sky that was to be darkened, before the day was out, by a storm that came perilously near to wrecking the entire enterprise.

As soon as possible I sought out crews and pilots for interview, only to find everywhere nothing but angry, frustrated men.

Not one of them had a story to tell for the simple reason that there was no story to tell. Not a single German fighter had left the ground that morning in answer to our attack. The difficulty of defending a perimeter as vast as that which Hitler held from the Atlantic coast of France up to the Baltic is that in addition to not knowing where exactly the invader will assault you it is virtually impossible to decide, in the early stages of attack, whether the first strike is a feint or the real thing. To commit yourself too soon in these circumstances could be tragic folly. Goering had therefore not committed either himself or his fighters: hence my furious, frustrated Canadians, denied the blood and battle they had waited so long to taste.

Nevertheless a despatch had to be written and sent off by plane to Air Ministry by mid-afternoon. At first I conceived the task of writing a despatch about nothing to be utterly hopeless; then I woke to the fact that the very nothingness of it was of high significance. Accordingly I dashed off the piece, took it to catch the special Air Ministry plane at four o'clock and then crossed my fingers. Less than a couple of hours later a delighted Dudley Barker was on the phone to me, warm in his praise of a piece I had considered hopeless.

For a week or more I wrote a despatch every day. As invasion progressed there was more and more action to cover and my confidence in my ability to cover it grew in parallel. Every piece was well received in London and I have rarely enjoyed an assignment more. If its beginnings had been clouded by apprehension its end had given me some of the satisfaction of 'something attempted, something done, has earned a night's repose'.

Our foothold on Europe having been secured it was reasonable now to begin to think in terms of the war's end. In fact a whole year was to go by, a great deal of it bloody and bitter, before it did end and for my own part there lay ahead of me an adventure totally unlike anything I had experienced before and which was to make the year 1945 the most significant of my life, in some ways, since that damp January day when I had walked into Bedford Square to meet Edward Garnett.

Before I tell of this particular and exciting adventure, however, I must deal with another which, though briefer and less significant in its effects, nevertheless had its own measure of excitement.

IV

Some time before D-Day at last occurred I had been home in Kent on leave for two or three days when I woke in the middle of the night to a great and hideous noise and the sight of what was clearly a burning aircraft flying low over the roof of the house. I had never before seen a burning aircraft flying so low at night but within minutes it was followed by another and then another and yet another. All were flying in the same direction, that is north-westwards, towards London, at the same height and with the same hideous racket. I was greatly mystified and, with four young children in the house, not a little frightened.

Morning solved the mystery; these were the first of Hitler's malevolent flying bombs, aptly named doodle-bugs, launched in formidable numbers, without respite, and with the object of causing infinite disaster to London and infinite damage to the morale of the civilian population. The flying bomb has been called an instrument of despair on the part of Hitler, who undoubtedly cherished the notion that what the blitz of 1940–41 had failed to achieve the impersonal evil machine of 1944 would. Undoubtedly he saw it as a softening-up device preceding the inevitable Allied invasion of the Continent. Equally undoubtedly we were unprepared for it (by 'we' I mean the civilian population; authority may have had its own information) and were taken greatly by surprise. It was not long, however, before we learned to listen for the sinister cut-out of the bug's power, the dreaded after-silence and the final inevitable bang: moments which were not funny but which had about them a dark and chilling air of doom.

At first our defences against these evils were badly deployed. For a few days London bore the blistering brunt of the attack and then defence chiefs moved quickly. It was swiftly realized that doodle-bugs must be intercepted either before they reached

England's southern coast-line or in the immediate hinterland between the coast and the neighbourhood of the North Downs. Fighter squadrons were accordingly re-deployed and pilots suddenly found themselves engaged in a riotous and unreal sort of circus in which they were fighting an enemy as impersonal and ghoulish as any robot. The doodle-bug in fact proved easy meat and many were the devices said to have been used by pilots for knocking them down, one being the use of a fighter's wing-tip to flip the bug off balance and send it reeling on its earthward way.

This is not to say that the bugs did not do untold damage; nor to deny that the populace were very frightened, wearied and highly tense from nervous strain, irritation and lack of sleep. Nor was London alone in this; the Kentish countryside had the unenviable experience of being the graveyard of thousands of bugs shot down before they reached the capital. A shot-down bug was not, of course, a dead bug; as it hit the earth, whether in cornfield, village street, meadow or church-yard, it exploded just the same, all too often with fatal results. On my own piece of pastoral England more than 3,000 of these intercepted bugs fell in a few weeks, so that a map showing each fallen bug looks like a settlement of black flies on a dead carcass. Perhaps the most remarkable of these was one which on a beautiful July evening floated over my house, cut out half a mile away and fell after the usual sinister silence with an almighty bang, having ended its flight on the top of the church tower under which, so many years before, Madge and I had paused to watch a flock of sheep safely graze. The moment was a doubly sad one, since Little Chart Church was, unless I am gravely misinformed, the only Protestant church in England that contained within its walls a Roman Catholic chapel. Today the ruined and empty tower stands as a stark grey monument to one of war's more senseless stupidities.

From all this racket and tension I was immensely relieved, in August, to be given a couple of weeks' leave. We accordingly went to Scotland, where Edinburgh's calm and beauty formed a haven of bliss after the dreary dread and gloom of the South.

The Trossachs seemed as lovely as the very Elysian fields and Edinburgh itself seemed hardly to know that a war was on, let alone that London and the South were living out a nightmare. For me, however, the respite was short-lived. After a few days there arrived from Dudley Barker a telegram ordering me immediately back to London. As I received it I instantly remembered my friend the hotelier's injunction about never arriving anywhere on time and I decided that 'immediately' meant at least another twelve hours. This was eminently sensible, since to have caught a morning train would merely have meant arriving in the capital at night, when all but air-raid wardens and their various brethren would have gone to bed. Far more sensible to catch the night train and arrive for breakfast, which I accordingly did, only to be woken in the dead of night by a guard calling 'Squadron-Leader Bates, Squadron-Leader Bates!' and ultimately to be handed a second telegram, couched in terms considerably more severe than the first.

I confess to fearing some extremely stern reprimand when I turned up, sleepy-eyed and not at all well-shaven, at Air Ministry that morning; but Dudley Barker, most amenable of men, had no word of reproach to offer and merely informed me that he wished me to fly to France on a mission the sole object of which was to seek out, and report on, doodle-bug launching sites in the area of Picardy and the Pas de Calais. I was to take all the time I wanted, go where I wanted and, if I thought fit, as Dudley obligingly put it, have a look at Paris while I was there.

I departed from Northolt the following afternoon in the usual tin-can Dakota. My wretched stomach, never any good at the best of times, revolted violently on the flight and I was miserably sick for most of the journey, which finally ended at Amiens, where groups of the French Resistance Movement were still rounding up sorry-looking bands of Nazi prisoners from the surrounding woodlands. Presently I was piling into a truck with various other officers and men, to be driven out of Amiens to an encampment on the town's outskirts. All was

Little Chart
Church

infinitely dreary; the camouflaged tents might have been prisons; the food, if food it could be called, was ghastly.

Happily I fell in with an Australian Air Force officer, who turned out to be as depressed as I was. 'I can't bear this bloody place,' he said. *'I want to smell France. The real France.'* These were thoughts so much after my own heart that I suggested we beg, borrow or steal some kind of transport and go and spend the night in Amiens. This we accordingly did, finding ourselves a room in a crumbling little hotel which I strongly suspect was also a brothel. However, we slept well and, as my Australian friend had so devoutly wished, smelled the real smell of France again: and very good to smell it was.

Early next day I set out to seek transport for the purpose of executing my doodle-bug mission. There was no transport. I then discovered a young R.A.F. driver who informed me, with a confidence and assurance that would have done credit to my old friend the hotelier, that of course there was transport. He could lay his hands on a jeep in no time; you just had to know. Within a quarter of an hour he was back with the promised jeep and I was, as I thought, on my way to the early execution of my mission. I was, as it turned out, almost on my way to another kind of execution, since we had scarcely driven half a mile when we were abruptly halted by two service policemen who irately demanded to know what the Hell we were doing with the Group-Captain's jeep? I duly sought out the Group-Captain and proceeded to eat, before him, the largest piece of humble pie I have ever had to consume.

All this, however, did little or nothing to deter my young driver, who in no time at all was back with another jeep, at the same time full of assurances that this time it had not been filched from higher authority. So we set off, not knowing quite what we were looking for or where to look for it. My French, far less adequate even than it is now, helped a little but not much as we stopped a peasant here and a peasant there in order to make our needs known. Finally we tracked down the first of our flying-bomb launching sites.

It was of almost frighteningly simple construction, consisting as it did of two lengths of railway line poised in the air at an angle of 45°. Up this track the doodle-bug was launched, to float away, if all went well, in the direction of England. Often, in fact, all did not go well. Not infrequently the doodle-bug stalled, spun backwards and fell back on its unfortunate launchers, blowing them to exceedingly small pieces. On other occasions a bug would execute a much larger loop, falling on the equally unfortunate citizens of Amiens, with similarly ghastly results.

These launching pads were all of identical construction. The only difference was in the sites they occupied. Some were well hidden in woods; others in orchards; a few in back gardens; and one at least occupied a village street. I suppose, that morning, I saw and inspected perhaps twenty of them, arriving at last at the conclusion, fortified by complete boredom, that having seen one I had seen them all. It must have been about two o'clock when I finally decided that the sight of one more doodle-bug site would drive me scatty and I remembered the words of Dudley Barker.

'Ever been to Paris?' I asked my young driver.

'No, sir. Never.'

'Well, you're going now.'

We drove southward. If I thought that the road to Paris was to be an easy one I was shortly to be much disillusioned. I

knew, but had failed fully to appreciate the fact, that every bridge in France had been blown up in order to frustrate the Nazi retreat; but it was not until we reached our first river that I came to a moment of an awful realization that it was one thing to decide to go to Paris but quite another to get there. On either side of the river there appeared to be utter chaos: groups of service-men, French citizens carrying bundles, bags of all kinds of motley belongings wrapped in newspaper and so on. There appeared to be no hope whatever of getting across that river.

Then to my infinite surprise I saw a pontoon consisting of several insecure-looking planks lashed to empty petrol drums slowly being punted on its way across stream from the opposite bank. This was a welcome enough sight in itself; but what was even more welcome and astonishing was the sight of a beautiful woman standing on the pontoon, beside a black Citroën car, waving a bottle of brandy. Clearly she was very excited.

'Hullo there, England!' she shouted, in English. 'Lovely to see you! Have a brandy.'

As the pontoon touched the shore she leapt to the bank, excitedly waving the brandy bottle, and at once proceeded to embrace me with rapturous fervour. Her charm and vivacity and her unmistakable Englishness were matched only by her husband's charm and courtesy and his equally unmistakable Frenchness.

'First time we've been able to leave Paris since the occupation.' She first introduced herself as a Countess and then inquired where I was bound for. When I said Paris her excitement mounted. Where was I going to stay? When I said that I hadn't the remotest idea she at once said: 'Then you must stay at our apartment. The concierge and his wife will look after you and will be thrilled to have you. I'll write down the address. It's in the Place des Etats Unis, just off the Avenue Kléber, not far from the Etoile.'

We drank more brandy; she wrote down her address; and then I asked where she and her Count were going.

'To our Château. Not far from Amiens. Haven't seen it

since 1940. Will you be coming back that way?' I said that I supposed we would. 'Then you must call and stay with us there. I insist. No formalities. Just drop in. God, it's great to speak to an Englishman again.'

We parted, brandy-filled, as rapturously as we had met, she warmly insistent that we used her apartment in Paris and equally urgent that we call on her at her northern Château. I promised fervently to do both and then we drove on our respective ways.

As we approached Paris, however, I began to have misgivings. Had the Countess been talking or was it the brandy? On cooler reflection I decided it was the brandy and in consequence told my young driver to take me to the Hotel Scribe. This, as I understood it, was being used as a centre for radio and newspaper correspondents and innocently I trusted I should find some kind of succour there. Instead I found a madhouse. Nobody knew anything about anything. Nobody had time either to speak or listen. All was bedlam and chaos.

Then by pure chance I ran into Richard Dimbleby. Though I didn't know him personally but only by reputation I knew

D 49

that he knew my agent, Laurence Pollinger, very well. I accordingly introduced myself, explaining at the same time that I could get no change out of anybody and that I had nowhere to sleep.

'You must bang the bloody table!' said Richard. 'It's the only way to get anything done in this damn place.'

By this time I was more than a little weary and in no mood for table-banging. There was nothing for it, therefore, but to navigate to the Place des Etats Unis.

This square, I should explain for the benefit of those who do not know it, is one of the most exclusive in Paris, and much of my apprehension returned as we drew up to the Countess'

Place des Etats Unis

grand establishment. I need not, however, have worried. The joy on the faces of the concierge and his little wife was comparable only with that of the Biblical shepherd rejoicing over his one lost sheep that had at last been found. Fortunately I was armed with a plentiful supply of 'K' rations and a pound or two of real coffee. This in itself was pure gold and soon, in return for it, the wife of the concierge was cooking us an omelette as only the French know how to.

But before this she showed us up to our rooms. I have rarely seen anything in such palatial, perfect taste. Rare Persian rugs, fine old masters, exquisite china and glass, sumptuous period furniture: I felt myself to be in a miniature Renaissance palace.

One thing, however, disturbed me. To my considerable consternation Madame now and then referred to a 'Monsieur Barker'. Did she, in some way, know about Dudley; or did Dudley know about me and my tendency to truancy? I failed to decide. Then by chance the word 'Granville' was dropped to join 'Barker' and the mystery was solved. The sumptuous apartment really belonged to the celebrated Granville Barker, man of the theatre.

Next day the wife of the concierge was insistent that I meet the wife of another concierge. Madame Martin, who lived on the far side of the Place des Etats Unis, was, it seemed, English, though her husband was a Frenchman. Great would be her joy at meeting an officer of the Royal Air Force.

That afternoon I accordingly went to call on Madame Martin and found a tiny red-haired woman whose diminutive stature perfectly matched the tiny concierge rabbit hutch in which she and her husband, like thousands of others of their kind in Paris, somehow existed on the ground floor. The pathetic nature of this tiny box contrasted painfully with a house where grandeur was even more palatial than that of the house of Monsieur Barker. But of Madame Martin's joy there was no shadow of doubt. Her red letter day, long prayed and hoped for, had at last arrived. With touching, tearful insistence she begged that I would take tea with her; and take tea I did, the tea being made from a few pathetic ounces jealously hoarded ever since the Nazi legions had triumphantly tramped into Paris.

As we took tea Madame Martin referred on several occasions to *la Duchesse*. It was the greatest pity that *la Duchesse* was away in the country. *La Duchesse* would have been greatly honoured and delighted to have met an English officer. In her excitement Madame Martin frequently forgot her English, the opportunity to speak which had been denied her for nearly five years, and lapsed into a mongrel language composed of three parts French to one of almost broken English, so that sometimes I had difficulty in understanding her.

Many years later I saw her again. The occasion was one at which my French publishers were giving a cocktail party in honour of a new book of mine. The *rendezvous* was in the Place des Etats Unis and great was Madame Martin's astonishment when I walked into her tiny rabbit hutch and handed my hat and coat to her. But greater still was my surprise to find that my hostess was *la Duchesse* herself. I will refrain from giving her name but will be content merely to record that it was that of one of France's most renowned and aristocratic families. Not that it is she I remember. The figure that still haunts my mind is that of the tiny Madame Martin, with her red hair and precious ounces of tea, by no means happily married to her French husband, living a life of virtual imprisonment under conditions that many an animal lover would have found intolerable for a dog, her life sweetened at last by liberation and the sharing of a cup of tea with an English officer. Somehow she personifies France's war-time agony more deeply than any Frenchwoman could have done, just as *la Comtesse*, so rabidly English, personifies her joy.

I cannot now recall with any accuracy how long we stayed in Paris. My acutest and most abiding memory is of wandering, in a hazy day-dream, by the Seine, stopping to browse over book-stalls or to chat with an occasional fisherman and then of wandering up and down the Rue de Rivoli, the windows of whose shops were astonishingly filled with goods that had long since disappeared from England.

Finally, with fond farewells, we left for the north. As we drove out of Paris we saw, at every street corner, hordes of hungry faces – hungry not for food but for a lift to somewhere out of Paris. As the jeep would hold only one extra passenger I decided that the fairest thing to do was to give a lift to no one, a resolution in which I was frustrated by a young woman who athletically leapt into the vehicle while it was moving, shouting, 'Lille, Lille, Lille!'

In vain I told her that I was not going to Lille and that I had certainly no intention whatever of doing so. She implored me, in typical Gallic fashion, to change my mind. I was quite adamant. She then offered me money. I declined more firmly than ever. Then, as we again reached the river where *la Comtesse* had jubilantly waved her brandy bottle at me, she begged me to walk along the river bank with her while we waited for the pontoon to cross. We walked as far as a stretch of woodland and here, as she paused, I realized that if only I would take her to Lille another kind of bribe could be mine for the taking. This too I very firmly declined and we finally left her in a state of tearful and angry frustration on the riverside.

Some few miles farther north we then came upon a sad sight. A young man and woman, bearing a long stout pole from one pair of shoulders to another, were wearily plodding along

53

a road as long and straight and barren as only certain French roads can be, the pole bearing two large and clearly very weighty suitcases. The pair looked fit to drop. The good Samaritan in me that had with apparent callousness rejected the girl from Lille, rose up at once, greatly touched. We stopped the jeep and the exhausted couple fell into the back.

'*Où allez-vous?*' I said in my primitive French.

'*Amiens.*'

'*Moi aussi.*'

The noises from the back of the jeep were a strange chorus of tears and laughter.

As we drove on they explained that they had left Paris riding a single ancient bicycle – a machine which, under the prodigious combined weight of two grown people and two vast suitcases, had promptly and inevitably broken clean in half.

So we took them to Amiens, where they too, like Madame Martin, had hoarded a few precious ounces of tea, which we now gratefully shared with them, at the same time declining an offer of an evening meal and a bed for the night.

'No,' I said to my young driver, 'we have to get on.'

'Where to now, sir?'

'We are,' I said, 'going to call on the Countess.'

We duly found the Château of the Countess, a typically grey turreted house of the kind to be seen all over France, only

to discover that there was, alas, no Countess. From below the low hillside on which the Château stood there were, however, sounds of village revelry, and it was here, the servants of the Château informed us, that we should find the Countess, dancing.

The astonished Countess, vastly enjoying herself at a village hop, was even more jubilant and excited at seeing us than when she had first waved the brandy at me from the pontoon. She at once insisted on leaving the dance and repairing to the Château, there to kill, if not the fatted calf, at least a bottle or two of precious wine. This we did and very soon the four of us were sitting down to an extremely good dinner, we full of our gratitude for all the hospitality at the Place des Etats Unis, she eager to hear how we had found the people and the city. I had in fact been greatly excited by the city; so much so that many subsequent visits to Paris have never quite matched my simmering fervour on that first post-war, or almost post-war, return. The evening continued and ended gaily.

Memory again serves me poorly here, since I find myself quite unable to remember if we spent one, two or three nights at the Château. I recall only that it was all infinitely pleasant, that I promised I would telephone the Countess's father when I got back to England and that finally, when we did leave, I went away burdened with gifts that seemed comparable with those borne by the three Wise Men, among them a superlative handbag for my wife. There was further a parting injunction that we shouldn't fail, on any account, to visit an Anglophile friend of the Count and Countess, some fifteen miles away. She too was a Countess and her arms, we were assured, would be open to infinite widths to receive us.

Having enjoyed the company of one countess so much, we had no hesitation in seeking out the second. This we quickly did, to discover that her house was not a Château, in the grey, turreted, almost prison-like French tradition, but a big four-square stone manor house, a true French farm *manoir* built round a huge central stone-flagged courtyard. Here, when we arrived, a number of women servants were sitting in the evening sunlight on hard kitchen chairs, very much in the French summer fashion, knitting, sewing and gossiping. After I had introduced myself my primitive French once again elucidated the fact that, alas, *la Comtesse* was not at home. However, I was assured, she soon would be and would we be pleased to wait?

I spent the waiting time wandering in the huge, square, typically stone-walled garden. Here, on the walls, glowed ripe crimson peaches of luscious magnificence; I fancy there were also deep purple figs; and in glass frames there shone, like green-gold suns, cantaloupe melons of such opulence that you felt they must surely burst and, like over-full cornucopia, spill out their golden juicy riches. Seeing it all I began to have certain doubts as to whether in fact the French had starved under the German yoke or if some, if not all of them, had lived in little insulated rural paradises, lushly as medieval nobles: a suspicion that, as I shall presently explain, was well supported next day.

In due course Countess No. 2 arrived: a rather older woman than the first but equally attractive, equally excited, equally delighted to have the honour of entertaining an English officer. It was she who graciously took us into the house which, inside, was even more a true French *manoir* than it appeared from the courtyard. Vast rooms, vast beams, vast doors, a vast oak refectory table laid for supper: it might all have come straight out of some story by Maupassant. One felt in it the very breath of a France feudal, burdened with a centuries-old rural tradition, self-contained and self-supporting, cut off not only from any urban, outside world but from that more sinister one of Nazi occupation.

These first impressions of mine grew stronger and stronger as we collected round the great refectory table for supper. What further astonished me was the extraordinary number of people who had now gathered for the evening meal. It was not merely that we were suddenly *en famille*, with *grand'mère*, *tante* this and *tante* that, the Count and Countess and a sister or two, but there was also the farm bailiff and several other retainers whose exact *rôles* were not clear to me. Again the scene might have been one out of a story by Maupassant;

again, as in the garden, there was no hint of things impecunious or impoverished; you felt indeed that war and all its attendant trials and atrocities had passed this lovely *manoir* and its opulent oasis completely by.

In the morning, at breakfast, my suspicions about the fullness or emptiness of at least some French bellies under Nazi occupation were finally and fully confirmed. In the centre of the big breakfast table I found myself gazing on a large square yellow object weighing perhaps two or three pounds. After gazing at it for some minutes in wonder and disbelief I was at last moved to inquire what it was. '*C'est du beurre, naturellement.*'

Butter! A block of not much less than three pounds of it. Fresh farmhouse butter. I couldn't recall ever having seen so much butter before except long ago when, as a boy, I used to go for my mother to the local dairy, there to watch with fascination the white-coated attendant slicing lumps of butter from a great block and smacking it into shapes with wooden pats on cold marble counters. But in war-time – the thing was a mocking miracle. The piece of butter on the breakfast table seemed soon to assume the size of a yellow tombstone and I could only wonder how large an English family, pitifully eking out its meagre rations, it would have fed and for how long.

I was then further moved to tell the Countess that I had never, or at least for a very long time, seen so large a quantity of butter: an admission which seemed to amuse her much. I was then emboldened to ask if I couldn't, perhaps, buy a pound or two of it in the village to take back to England with me.

'Today it is doubtful. Today is not a butter-making day. But tomorrow will be. So if you will stay with us another night – and we do hope that you will – we will round up a decent quantity for you. I hope you will stay for another reason – I know that some of the French Resistance boys would be greatly honoured to meet you.'

I duly met some half dozen of the French Resistance boys – and they were really not much more than boys – who promptly invited me to lunch with them in Amiens the following day.

We were to meet at midday in the central square. I was very happy to accept but breakfast the next morning made me happier still: for there, waiting for me, was my miracle of butter, about four pounds of it, together with a great box of luscious peaches, several melons and a number of pairs of pure silk stockings for my wife. I don't think I wept at the sight of these riches, but I am not ashamed to confess that as I said farewell to the Countess, her opulent garden and her Maupassant-like *manoir* I was very near to tears.

At midday, having met the French Resistance boys, I was taken off by them to a modest and typically plebeian restaurant called *Restaurant des Cultivateurs et Voyageurs*. And here, once again, I found my suspicions about French bellies well confirmed. Having eaten a large and excellent dish of *tomates provençal*, I was just preparing to relax, fully replete, when I was astonished, if not indeed dismayed, to discover that this was merely what is sometimes called a starter. To follow *les tomates* there arrived an equally large and equally excellent dish of *blanquette de veau*, with which I confess my poor war-shrunken stomach found it hard to cope.

That afternoon, laden with riches and feeling almost as if returning homeward from some fabulous Samarkand instead of from a France stricken and divided, I hitched a lift on the beer-plane to England. I name it the beer-plane because that is precisely what it was: a small hedge-hopping machine, probably a D. H. Rapide, which jumped from one air-field to another, depositing crates of beer and taking empties away.

My trip had been one of much reward and excitement. If I hadn't learned much of great importance about doodle-bug launching sites I had learned, or had more truly confirmed for myself, much else. The descriptions of rural France in *Fair Stood the Wind For France* had had necessarily to be done, almost all of them, from imagination. Now my visit had proved, not for the first or last time, that imagination can take a writer nearer to the heart of truth than any amount of observation, and that instinct, rather than sheer reasoning, will often guide him just as surely. Once again indeed Thackeray's celebrated dictum had been justified: 'the work of fiction contains more truth in solution than the work which purports to be all true.'

I had now ahead of me another adventure, larger and of far wider import than the mere interlude in France; and of this I must now proceed to tell.

V

As the winter of 1944–45 came on my health grew infinitely worse. The abdominal pains I had had to endure with increasing misery since my schooldays had now become a scourge. Pain not only tortured me by day, but kept me agonisingly awake at night. I wrote little of any consequence and derived little or no pleasure from what I did. It was clear that one day surgeons would have 'to take a little peep' inside me but no such operation would be possible until a more critical stage in my physical condition had been reached. I simply had to grin and bear it.

When therefore Dudley Barker summoned me to his desk at Air Ministry one day in mid-January 1945 it was to greet me with something like these words:

'We all know what a miserable time you've been having with your health and if you want to say "No" to the proposition I'm going to put to you we shall all understand. It's entirely up to you. If you feel you must decline please decline. Nothing more will be said.'

'What is the proposition?'

'We'd like you to go to Burma. You would actually be based in India, at Calcutta, where Doddie will look after you.'

'How long for?'

'Entirely up to you. The object of the exercise is to write half a dozen pieces – even some short stories – specifically for the American market. It's felt that the Americans should be made aware that there is in fact a war going on in Burma, and a pretty desperate one at that. But, as I say, you don't *have* to go. It's neither a posting nor an order.'

'May I think it over?'

'That's exactly what we want you to do. In fact buzz off now, talk it over with your wife and tell us later what you feel. But remember – there's no compulsion.'

Oddly enough, I felt excited. My feelings were very much akin to those I had experienced when Hilary Saunders, Harald Peake and John Nerney had first proposed that I should be commissioned into the R.A.F. solely to write short stories. Here, now, was a new field to explore, a new theatre from which I might extract stories and drama. Once again I felt excited, honoured and no little apprehensive.

For a day or two I talked it over with Madge and she, like me, felt it was clearly my duty to accept the proposition. She knew that, with four very young children, my absence would be hard for her; and I knew it too. But neither of us ever really felt otherwise than that I should go to India and Burma, and within another day or so I went back to Dudley Barker to tell him so.

Dudley, though pleased at my decision, nevertheless warned me: 'We probably won't be able to get you away before early February, so if in the meantime you decide to change your mind you are perfectly free to do so.'

I replied that I didn't think I would change my mind and I may even have said – I certainly thought it – that healthwise the trip might even do me good. The only further comment I had from Dudley was the simple one that 'India is a mess'. Little did I know.

So on a day in early February Madge came with me to B.O.A.C.'s air terminal in London, where we said a fond but rather dejected farewell. Scarcely had she waved her hand for the last time and disappeared into the street than a loud-speaker announcement told that my flight had been cancelled. I was home ten minutes after Madge and we were able to have one more evening together.

Next day I entrained for Swindon and thence to Lyneham. There a positive horde of service-men and women had been waiting for an entire week for February's fogs to clear and they were full of mocking laughter at the new buoyant contingent just arriving. Nevertheless, that night, the fog did clear; morning broke white with hoar-frost and by half past eight we were air-borne. An hour or two later I could see the far

61

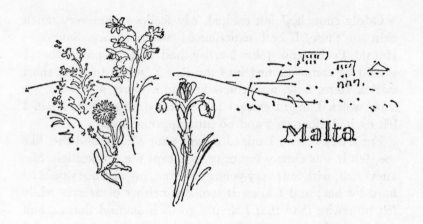

Malta

distant line of the Alps, looking like a crowd of pink sugar mice nestling together in the low, brilliant morning sun.

Eventually, on the dark blue sea below, a rock appeared: of such apparent and unexpected smallness that I simply couldn't believe that this was our first stop, Malta. But Malta it was and soon half a dozen of us were wandering among Valletta's white and sparkling ruins. Malta indeed was a sad sight; there was little to do or buy; and we ended the day by taking a moth-eaten gharry and driving to some remote black market restaurant and there eating what I strongly suspect was some species of dog heavily flavoured with garlic and herbs. If however I give the impression that Malta was a scene of utter desolation I must at once correct it. Its ruins apart, it was a little paradise of flowers; arum lilies, narcissi, irises, stocks, sweet-peas, marigolds and trees of fruit blossom. I marvelled and revelled greatly in that premature touch of spring.

Next morning we flew on to Cairo, arriving in time for a lunch which my tiresome stomach rejected, so that I spent most of the time slowly sucking at an orange and gazing dreamily at a vase of sweet-peas. After lunch, since our flight wasn't due to continue until the small hours of the morning, six of us, including I think two army brigadiers, thumbed a lift in a truck and made for Cairo. One had the immediate impression that that city had been shipped straight from

Paradise. I recall a shop window full of sponges, a sight which so awed and transfixed us that we spent an unconscionable amount of time simply staring at it in total disbelief, not like a group of grown men but like schoolboys outside a tuck-shop long out of bounds. Then there was the famed *confiserie* of Mr Groppi, sparkling with riches long denied us: chocolates, cakes, tarts, sweetmeats of every kind. Here we didn't merely gaze; the latent schoolboys in us leapt to life, positively falling over each other with mouth-watering greed. Finally we discovered – the city now as brilliantly lit as a fair – a restaurant in which two dozen chickens revolved on a spit over a glowing charcoal fire. Small wonder that we drove back to base more than a little heady on Palestinian wine.

Cairo

We flew off in early morning darkness. I invariably find it impossible to sleep in an aircraft and I sat awake for several hours, merely staring at the blackness ahead. Suddenly the

63

blackness sparkled with jewels: diamonds, rubies, emeralds. This was our airfield; we were about to come down in Persia.

Dawn was breaking as we touched down; then we washed, shaved and breakfasted briefly. Sheiba airfield looked like any other airfield in the middle of a desert: sandy, wind-swept, desolate. This in fact was my one and only glimpse of Persia, yet many years later I had the strangest dream: I dreamed that I was a magistrate-cum-tax collector in a small remote Persian town and that I was to preside over the magistrates' court. The year was 200 B.C. (this perhaps was the oddest part of the dream, since one couldn't know, in 200 B.C. that in fact it was B.C.). Another vivid fact was the blinding, blistering heat of the day: a fact that made me decide to start holding the court immediately after dawn. Still more vivid was the sight of the shadows in the narrow Persian streets shrinking and shrinking until, at midday, under the perpendicular sun, they existed no longer.

The first strange thing about this dream is that, unlike so many dreams, it has never faded; it still has the same indelible brilliance as on the night when I first experienced it. The second strange thing is that I had not, beforehand, been reading or talking of Persia or seeing anything of the country on the television screen. My entire acquaintance with Persia consisted solely of one hour, in war-time, on an R.A.F. airfield. How to explain it all? My friend Ann Todd, the actress, a woman of much intelligence, entertains no shadow of doubt about it. I *was* once a Persian magistrate and am now reincarnated.

After Persia we flew on to Karachi. My first experience of India (this was before the birth of Pakistan) was to drink the vilest cup of tea that has ever passed my lips and as I threw it away my heart for some reason, sank to my boots. I suddenly felt bitterly, depressingly homesick, a sensation that wasn't in any way lessened by the fact that when the aircraft took off again I found myself to be the one remaining passenger. The fact of that isolation, as we flew over India's vast desert interior, filled me with a dark and desolate gloom.

We came in to land, stickily, in a cross-wind at Dum-Dum

airfield. Perhaps it was merciful that Dudley's comment
'India is a mess' had remained cryptic and unexpanded. I knew,
in fact, nothing of India; its history had largely passed me by;
I hated Kipling; of the sub-continent's many languages and
dialects I had heard only of Hindi, of its rivers only the Ganges.
Ignorance may indeed, at times, be bliss, but as I stepped out
into the afternoon's torrid heat on Dum-Dum's tarmac there
was to be no bliss for me.

Nor was I suffering merely from ignorance. I cherished
several fond if not idiotic illusions. One was that Doddie, if
unable to meet me himself, would surely have sent someone,
with the necessary transport, in his place. I soon realized that
there was in fact no Doddie and no transport. Desperate inquiry
at several offices purporting to be sections of the R.A.F.
merely brought, from young Indian servicemen, that curious
sideways tilt of the head that seems to indicate something half
way between yes and no but which experience finally teaches
simply means damn-all. I then realized that I hadn't the
faintest idea where Doddie's Headquarters were; nor had I
fully grasped the fact that the day was Saturday, nor the still
more discomforting fact that in Calcutta the war stopped,

every Saturday, at noon. All I knew, or thought I knew, was that Doddie was somewhere in Calcutta, then a city of $4\frac{1}{2}$ million people and some twenty-five miles in diameter. This in fact was another fond illusion, since Group-Captain Dodds was, in fact, not in Calcutta but in Hastings, twenty miles northward up the River Hooghli. Nor did I then know that the reason why neither Doddie nor anyone else had come to meet me was that authority – and this at a time when it was almost as difficult to get out of England as out of Wormwood Scrubs – had neglected to include me on the manifest of any aircraft leaving England during the three previous days. Officially I was lost.

By this time I also felt personally lost. Eventually I hitched a lift in a truck going into Calcutta, the centre of which, another fact I didn't know, was twenty miles away. In a recent article a celebrated journalist has called Calcutta the most degraded and disgusting great city in the world, a description the full taste of which I was to savour as I now drove through twenty miles of what are indisputably some of the most revolting, most stinking, most rat-ridden, most sickening and most depraved slums in the world. A dead cow rotting on the roadside in the grilling heat of afternoon, giving off the stench of putrefaction and the charnel house; a mad rush of gharries, cars and rickshaws; an old woman, a mere shrunken bag of bones, dying in the gutter without a soul bothering to spare her a second glance; a great mass of rotting filth choking every pavement, gully and alleyway; the evil stench of poverty, of hordes of unwashed bodies, of burning dung: these are merely a few of the more obvious, more odious, more sickening features of that seemingly endless journey through Calcutta's slums on that torrid afternoon.

Eventually the truck-driver dumped me, bed-roll, bags and all, on the pavement outside the Great Eastern Hotel, in the very centre of Calcutta. The hotel, used as a sort of transit camp, teemed with servicemen, a complete madhouse. Lost in utter bewilderment, I suddenly spotted an Air Commodore and asked him if he possibly knew where I might find Group-

66

Captain Dodds? He stared at me as if I had asked for Jesus Christ himself. I repeated the experience with several other people, always with the same result, until I suddenly knew, exhausted and drowned in sweat as I was, that I was going rapidly and irrevocably mad.

Presently, in this utterly desperate state, I spotted an R.A.F. sergeant in a jeep. I went over to him and begged, yet again, if he might possibly tell me where I could find Group-Captain Dodds.

'Dodds? Never 'eard of 'im. What mob's he in?'

'Public Relations.'

'Gor blimey, why didn't you say so the first time? 'Op in.'

I threw my kit into the back of the jeep and hopped in. We then drove crazily round several back streets, crushing watermelon rinds as we skidded round corners, honking at the usual press of dhoti-clad Indians, all looking like lazy brown-and-white moths. It was by now five o'clock and to my horror the sergeant suddenly muttered something about we'd be 'bleeding lucky if the office wasn't shut by now'. Eventually, however, we drew up in a narrow alley and the sergeant said:

'This is it. On the first floor. I'll keep an eye on your kit while you go up.'

Near to utter exhaustion, I crawled upstairs. At the head of them a thin Squadron-Leader, accompanied by a woman companion, was in the very act of locking an office door.

I introduced myself and he almost fainted.

'Good God, Laddie,' he said in strong Scots accent, 'we've been searching high and low for you all day. Where've you been? Do you not know you're not on the manifest of any aircraft that's left Great Britain for the past three days?'

No, I said, I didn't know; nor did I care.

At this point the Squadron-Leader introduced himself as Nickie, then his companion as Mrs Henderson. 'Mrs Henderson and her husband Tom are old friends of mine. Aye, they're Scots like me.'

I shook hands with Mrs Henderson, a small bright-eyed, cheerful woman who eyed me up and down keenly – purely because, as she afterwards explained, she simply couldn't believe that I could possibly be as weary as I looked.

'Talking of manifests,' I said, 'it's manifest that I get a room somewhere. Is there a hotel you can recommend?'

The Squadron-Leader laughed uproariously.

'Listen, Laddie. Calcutta's a city of four and a half million people and it has three hotels. One is a sort of transit camp, one is a brothel that when it isn't a brothel is closed because of dead dogs, cats or rats in the water supply. The other has so many bugs they eat you alive. Hotels? – you must be joking, Laddie. Joking.'

Then where the devil, I wanted to know, could I stay?

Mrs Henderson gave me another long, searching, pitying look. 'Ye dinna need worry your head about that tonight. My husband and I'll see ye have a bed for tonight.'

I thanked her warmly and a few minutes later I was piling my kit into the Squadron-Leader's car and the three of us were retracing the sordid miles of Calcutta's slums that had so sickened and revolted me an hour or so before. The second sight of them seemed only to reveal a greater squalor than the

first; the dead cow putrefying by the roadside had entered an even more evil, sickening state of putrefaction; on trees and fences about it vultures were already gathering, evil-looking themselves, in readiness for tomorrow's scavenging gorge; everywhere in bazaars and streets and alleyways there seemed to be greater crowds than ever; rickshaws, both man-powered and bicycle-powered, dashed precariously among huge open taxis, all driven by dark turbanned Sikhs; trotting, sweating coolies bearing loads on the ends of long poles, so that they looked like pairs of human scales; women with great bundles on their heads; all seemed noisier, more chaotic, more miserable to look upon.

After a long period of all this we came to a more or less open road bordered on each side by dusty bullock tracks along which both bullocks and water-buffaloes were lugging heavy wooden carts, lumbering like Biblical beasts through deep rainless dust. Above them great tall palms threw long shadows, their high motionless fronds looking as if cut out of black steel against a sky almost colourless in the last half hour of daylight preceding India's swift short twilight.

Presently we came to another squalid settlement with the everlasting crowds, among which barbers sat in gutters cutting their clients' hair, and the everlasting squalor. Then suddenly we halted at a pair of enormous wooden gates, which were duly flung open in obedience to irate honkings on the car horn. A pair of obsequious Indians salaamed as we passed through into a biggish courtyard, on three sides of which stood a prison-like factory. 'Jute,' said Mrs Henderson and I then remembered that jute was the main artery of Calcutta's life-blood.

On the other side of the factory flowed the wide stewy Hooghli, its far bank already glittering with a thin scattering of lights. On the near bank, taking advantage of the last daylight, a gang of kneeling Indian women and girls were planting grass on a newly prepared stretch of red-brown earth, dibbing in each green tuft swiftly, as rice is planted. Behind them it was possible to pick out the patch-work of previous days' plantings,

69

the nearest pale and wilting, the farthest already a brilliant emerald green.

The Hendersons' flat was on the first floor of a block over-looking the river. We climbed up an outside iron staircase, an Indian bearer, a boy of perhaps thirteen, lugging my kit up behind us. The flat was far from large and out of it appeared Tom Henderson, shortish, of typical Scots countenance, looking slightly but patiently aggrieved that his wife, as I discovered was her habit, had brought home yet another weary R.A.F. waif-and-stray who could not find himself a bed. Tom Hender-son had in fact lost an R.A.F. son by an earlier marriage at some earlier stage of the war and in consequence, like his wife, was ever-ready to play the good Samaritan.

'Will ye no be takking a wee chota peg, mon?' Mr Henderson said.

My weary brain failed signally to translate this sentence of thick Scots, with its peppering of Hindustani, into any kind of sense and in answer I could only stare stupidly.

'Tom means would you like a drink?' Mrs Henderson said and I came suddenly to my senses, causing laughter.

For the next half an hour I drank much gin-and-tonic, well iced, and nothing had ever tasted so good. As we drank, Nickie announced that I was a writer, a piece of information that caused great surprise to spring into Mrs Henderson's face, as if she were unable to believe that such a species not only existed but had actually appeared in her home. But being also a practical soul, she almost at once suggested that I would surely like a bath, to which I responded with something like:

'God, that would be Heaven.'

It was indeed Heaven and thus refreshed I went early to bed, at last to slumber like a child under my mosquito net.

I woke early next morning, shaved, bathed again and then went out on to the terrace of the Hendersons' flat. The scene laid before my eyes in that exquisite first hour or so after sunrise was the perfect example of the fact that 'distance lends enchant-ment to the view'. The far bank of the Hooghli lay bathed in a

70

soft, delicious, opalescent light, as from a 'faery land forlorn' its temples and towers and houses rising from an assortment of trees and palms in infinitely tender shades of pink and cream and green and yellow and even lavender. That there lay under this sublimely beautiful, ethereally unreal curtain a dark sink of putrefying squalor seemed totally fantastic. I could only wonder which had cheated me most, the evening of the previous day or the sweet opal loveliness of my first Indian sunrise.

India, ruthless as ever towards human life, soon mocked me with an answer. Just below me, in the river, beyond the new-planted grass, a pale object floated past, twisting in slow curves on the downstream current. It was the swollen body of a man, the first but by no means the last I was to see of the wide Hooghli's victims.

It wasn't long, however, before the first fond illusion of India's fairy dawn was to be burnt in the cauldron of rising day. In an hour or two the sun was scalding; by noon the flat was an oppressive oven in which I sweated and wolfed at iced gin-and-tonic like an exhausted animal at a stream. 'Och! this is nothing,' the Hendersons said. 'This is only February. We've no begun to warm up yet. This is really the winter.'

Afternoon wrapped me in a long siesta, from which I emerged to the blessed refreshment of tea flavoured with fresh green limes. Soon afterwards Nickie appeared, announcing his readiness to drive us all up river to Hastings, there to find Group-Captain Dodds. It was growing dark as we left in his car and the air was alternately sweet and noisome with the heavy fragrance of what may have been incense trees and the fires, in villages, of burning dung. Something about this combination of the sweet and the acrid very much depressed my spirits. Sunday in time of war, as any serviceman would tell you, was the week's worst day, when families are most missed and most thought of and homesickness sits on the heart like a grey blight. That first drive up the Hooghli on Sunday still lives with me, vivid and gloomy as ever.

Headquarters at Hastings was housed, as I think I am right in saying, in a converted jute-mill. Its personnel consisted, I should say, of ninety per cent American, the rest British. As always, the Americans lacked for nothing: iced beer, drinks of all kinds, a club-house, a bar opulently built of bamboo, and girls and all the rest of it. (There is a story telling of how, at one period of the war in New Guinea, the morale of American troops dropped far below zero. The cause of this phenomenon was searched for far and wide. More beer, more hamburgers, more jazz, more women – these and a score of other opiates were investigated and rejected. It was then discovered by chance that what the troops were pining for were the comic supplements to American newspapers. These were duly flown out by the thousand in special aircraft and morale immediately rose like a moon rocket.) Not that we, the poor British, with a beer ration of one can a month, had cause to grouse at American affluence. Though they sometimes behaved with that singular insularity that is one of their less endearing characteristics (I once spent a night sharing a dormitory with seven or eight American officers, not one of whom spoke to me, as if fearing that mere conversational contact with a Limey might prove unpleasantly contagious) they were on the whole generous to their poor relations, conferring on us generous gifts of beer, a drink I am not normally very fond of but which, in Calcutta's sweltering cauldron, was sheer nectar.

It was good to see my old Commanding Officer again and his dry humour caused my spirits to rise and sweeten. Tomorrow we would meet, lunch, talk, make plans; I must get myself effectively kitted out (I was still wearing my thick R.A.F. uniform and mightily uncomfortable it was) and he would show me where. He also reminded me that another colleague from P.R.3, an officer named Chadwick, was also in Calcutta, together with one or two others I had known in London, including the journalist Andrew Rice, so that soon there would be no lack of friends. Chadwick was also a member of the Bengal Club, then probably the most exclusive club in the world, so that at least one avenue of civilisation would possibly be open to me. There was also the Swimming Club, a blessed haven as it proved, and Doddie would see that I was made a member of that.

If I have given the impression that Calcutta was wholly and irremediably squalid I must now make some effort to correct it. The east side of Calcutta was, as with so many great cities, its worst; its West End, as with London, Paris and many other cities, was infinitely superior. Here there is a wide park-like space, the Maidan, in which stands Government House, built by Lord Wellesley in 1799 and closely modelled on the great Adam house, Kedleston Hall, in Derbyshire (it must be remembered that Calcutta was once the capital of India, before New Delhi was built, being preferred to its rival Bombay because of the prevalence of plague in Bombay, a disease from which Calcutta, for all the nastiness of its climate, was relatively free). Government House was, when I first saw it, not only a fine Adam-like pile in itself, but more glorious than Solomon himself in its vast brilliant garment of red, salmon and magenta bougainvillaea: an exotic and amazing sight. And as if this vivid lustre were not enough great beds of cannas, six feet or more tall, in scarlet, crimson, yellow, orange and pink, flaunted their trumpets on the emerald, well-watered lawns in front of the great house, like companies of severely drilled soldiery on stiff and solid guard.

Alongside the Maidan runs one of the most famous streets in the world, Chowringee, once a row of palatial mansions, but now more like another Knightsbridge, filled with shops large and fashionable. Behind this were streets of colonial houses and gardens of considerable wealth and charm. Nor, indeed, would it be true to say that all of Calcutta was poor. Its large port ensures that it is a city of great wealth; though, as so often happens, its wealth abides with the few, its poverty with the many.

There is no doubt, however, that the atmosphere of Calcutta was confused, enervating and parochial. Calcutta's sister in the world of jute is Dundee, a fact which meant that a considerable part of the British resident population of the Indian city came from the Scottish one. Some, like Tom Henderson, had been there for the better part of 40 years – 'and I'm tellin' ye, mon,' they were fond of saying, 'I still don't know India.'

Here, I realized after less than a couple of weeks' acclimatisation, was my problem. If residents of 40 years' occupation didn't know the sub-continent how was I to fare? The problem, I realized, was not wholly unlike that which had confronted me on my first acquaintance with Bomber Command. Now, as then, I found myself in a world totally unfamiliar to me, its idiom strange, its people apparently unapproachable; yet from this difficult and unpromising material it was my job somehow to extract and translate into lucid form articles and stories which would convey to far distant readers a picture of what India, and later Burma, were like in the turmoil of war. What had seemed a task of apparent simplicity – namely that of writing half a dozen short pieces for American consumption – now began to seem of disturbing complexity.

This is precisely what I had felt at Oakington, but there, fortunately, I was living with the battle and with the men who were fighting it. In parochial, steaming Calcutta, in spite of the presence of thousands of servicemen of innumerable nation-

alities, there was no battle. The war, on its several fronts, was not only far away; it might not have existed. Where, then, was my material coming from? I appeased my conscience a little in that direction by writing what I think was a vivid piece on Calcutta itself which was well enough received, writing it in the comparative cool and quiet of the Swimming Club, in the morning, when the club was virtually deserted. For the rest I knew that I had, as I had done at Oakington, to keep my ears cocked for those stray crumbs of gossip which are so often enough to set the imagination of writers on fire.

Presently one of these crumbs was unwittingly let fall at the Hendersons' flat. Evening after evening there used to appear there a man of perhaps forty or so, clearly of much experience in the East, apparently hard-bitten and without doubt a hard drinker. He struck me as being very much like a character out of Conrad, a writer on whom in my extreme youth I had been strongly suckled and whose interpretation of the East, both atmospherically and otherwise, had long seemed to me infinitely superior to both that of Kipling, the Imperialist, and Maugham, the pretended cynic who was often a sentimentalist in disguise and whose world was in many ways as narrow as that of Surbiton – as parochial as that of Calcutta itself.

The apparently hard-bitten visitor to the Hendersons' flat belonged neither to the Imperialistic nor suburban world. He generally arrived at the flat about six o'clock, when he would talk civilly and coherently for perhaps half an hour or so, during which time he would ferociously consume a positively fearsome quantity of liquor. As this began to work he became progressively more introspective, maudlin and then almost tearfully truculent, even abusive. I had never seen a man drink so much in so short a time or with less evident enjoyment; here, it seemed to me, was a man setting out either deliberately to destroy himself or to drown some undrownable sorrow or to expiate or try to forget some unforgettable personal disaster – a kind of wartime Lord Jim.

I was so troubled and mystified by all this that I was moved eventually to ask Mrs Henderson what lay behind it all. 'He was a planter in Burma,' she said, 'and he was on the long march to India when the Japs moved in.' Great though the disasters of that march had been, as I knew well enough, they hardly seemed to me to justify a sort of alcoholic death-wish. There must also lie in that distressed mind, it seemed to me, the bitter kernel of some greater, more personal disaster. And so it turned out. His sorrow – and sorrow it was, profound, bitter and unforgettable – rose from the fact that his personal bearer, a mere boy, had died on the journey. The severance of this deep personal bond, born of mutual love and loyalty, had had so great an effect on him that he had been crushed into a state of morbid melancholia.

From this bitter crumb there was eventually to emerge *The Jacaranda Tree*. The birth of that book, however, still lay some years ahead and for the moment all I could do was to let the seed lie dormant, though by no means dead, in the deeper recesses of my mind.

Meanwhile, as Doddie was presently to remind me, Burma itself was very much a reality. Did I feel prepared, he asked, to fly across and have a look-see? A large, formidable map of the country, a jam-like mess of purple and green, secretly told me I was not so prepared. There was in fact a certain chill in my heart. I had a discomforting feeling that I was about to go out into the wilderness and that I might never return. The prospect of such banishment seemed not only harsh; it had the further effect of making even steaming, sordid, insalubrious Calcutta seem like a piece of Heaven.

Naturally, however, I said that I was willing and ready to go, and a few days later I was flying out over the Bay of Bengal.

VI

Sometime before this event, however, I had had my one and only quarrel with a fellow officer: nothing more than a flaming, stand-up row with Nickie. Squadron-Leader Nickson was the arch-type of that kind of middle-rank officer who by virtue of that rank sets up his own personal kingdom which he then proceeds to rule by threats, fear and even terror, petrifying all of lesser rank. In Nickie's case Erks, Waafs, Indian clerks, bearers and drivers were all held in terrifying thrall. The king in his kingdom, ruling by shouting, abuse, invective, foul language and often sheer bullying, was a law unto himself, and woe betide any who dared think otherwise.

Among other things Nickie was in charge of P.R. transport, both in the air and on the ground. Accordingly I went to him to request that I be given a jeep, it having been sensibly recognised at Air Ministry that I should, and must, have my own transport. With this firmly promised arrangement Nickie flatly refused to comply. In vain I pointed out that this was an Air Ministry instruction. 'Jeep? Ye'll have no jeep here. I've no jeep to spare and even if I had ye'd not get it.' Again I protested strongly; again I insisted that these were Air Ministry promises and instructions; again Nickie yelled 'No jeep! I'm tellin' ye for the last time – no jeep.' It was then my turn to yell, livid with lost temper as well as being no little nauseated by the conduct of the petty king-dictator. Presently the air grew flaming hot, then molten, and it was only when it had cooled a little that I saw the virtues of reason and swept coldly out of the office.

Outside, with no hesitation, I commandeered the nearest truck in sight, and promptly ordered its Indian driver to take me to Doddie. He, being the sort of man he was, listened to me with good sense and reason, saw the cogency of my arguments and told me not to worry. He would telephone Nickie. He duly did so and I got my jeep next day.

In the aftermath of this tempestuous atmosphere I now had to approach Nickie again on the question of air transport to Burma. The king-tyrant was again unco-operative, indeed offensive. There were no aircraft, or if there were they were all completely full. A great number of transports were U.S.; others, in case I didn't know it, were being eaten by termites. It would be days and days, perhaps weeks, before anything could be found. I knew all this to be stalling, if not deliberate enmity, but I was both impotent and powerless to do anything and the king-tyrant knew it well. For some days afterwards I turned up every morning at Nickie's office to inquire after my passage, but always with the same result: no aircraft. Finally I got a seat on a Dakota, a Dakota so ancient, so rickety, so tied up with string and, unless I was much mistaken, so eaten by termites that it would surely never, I thought, make the passage from Bengal to the Arakan. Ever since that day I have in fact nurtured the unpleasant thought that Nickie, by that shambles of an aircraft, hoped to kill me.

But reach the Arakan, along the Burma coast, I eventually did. It was mid afternoon when I arrived on the wide dusty airfield, far beyond which, to the north, a range of mountains smouldered in a vast heat-haze. On the ground itself, as I stepped thankfully from the aircraft, the searing, blinding sun struck down on me like a blow from a mighty white-hot steam hammer. Never had I felt anything like it; even the heat of Calcutta seemed temperate by comparison.

I was then assailed by a mirage. The dusty, barren airfield seemed suddenly to flower. Then the flower became a woman, a white woman, tall, shapely, elegant, very beautiful. I could only stare and wonder. Such things simply didn't happen on remote, sizzling Asian airfields. Then she moved and walked and I knew that this was no mirage. She was, as it turned out, an actress who had flown in to entertain such few servicemen as were left in Akyab.

My *Encyclopaedia Britannica* describes Akyab as the third

79

largest port in Burma, lying on the coast where three fertile valleys, watered by the rivers Myu, Koladaing and Lemyu, reach the sea in an intricate network of tidal channels, creeks and islands. The hinterland is described as rich with forest, the fertile alluvian valleys yielding inexhaustible supplies of rice.

Alas, when I saw it on that first burning, blinding afternoon, Akyab and its fertile valleys presented only a scene of bitter desolation. No rice had grown there for three years or more; Akyab was a half-swallowed ruin – swallowed by Mother Nature in all her torrid tropical vigour. The jungle ruled and dominated all. Vines, creepers, trees, elephant-grass twice as tall as a man, bamboos, palms – fed by tropical suns and watered by monsoons, the once thriving port of Akyab had disappeared under a kind of corruptive natural splendour.

All this had on me an impact as powerful as that of the sun had been; it drove deeply and permanently into my conscious-ness. At the same time it provoked in me a singular sadness. India seemed a senseless, seething mess; yet I felt that Burma, by contrast, must have been simple, ordered and happy, its people gentle, charming and reserved. Now, like Akyab itself, it was a mere husk, a dusty ghost, its people like trousered and half-broken wanderers in a dream.

Little of apparent significance seemed to happen to me on that first Burma visit. I say 'seemed' advisedly, since once again it was little things that dropped into my mind and lay dormant there, waiting to germinate and flower at some distant, even far distant, date. A large, rambling temple outside which young Burmese boys were pouring a cement-like mixture into small moulds which when baked hard by the powerful sun turned out as miniature Buddhas; a pretty little Burmese girl sitting on the step of a bombed pagoda, playing with a lizard, at first gently, merely teasing it, then with deliberate cruelty, wounding and finally killing it. Little and apparently in-significant episodes, yet the one stuck in the mind as epitomising the futility of religion, the other as an exposure of all the callous futility of war. The second of these episodes haunted me so uneasily that I went immediately back to my small hot

tent and tried, before the brilliance of its impact faded, to get it down on paper, I hoped as my first short story of the East. Not a word resulted: for reasons which I shall later set out in detail.

I flew back to India some ten days or so later, to re-enact there the stupid and exhausting merry-go-round I had been through on the first day of my arrival. A young half terrified native truck driver drove me desperately round Calcutta's sleazy suburbs in an attempt to find, in the dingy darkness, the Hendersons' flat. Just as I knew that we were irrevocably lost and he seemed about to go berserk we were stopped by an R.A.F. sergeant M.P. in a jeep, who had the good sense to order the boy back to his unit and then kindly gave me a lift in the right direction in the jeep.

That crazy drive gave me, however, a chance to see another side of Calcutta: Calcutta by night. If I now used words of my own to describe it I might well be accused of biased and deliberate falsification. I will therefore content myself with quoting from a recent article describing not the Calcutta of 1945, but the Calcutta of 1970, a quarter of a century after every wall in India had *Quit India* scrawled across it and India's millions couldn't wait for the British Raj, the hated Western imperialist, to be driven out. After heading the article *Oh! Calcutta! World's Greatest Urban Disaster*, the writer goes on:

'Millions have the pavements as their home. Miles of streets are strewn with sleeping families at night. But the pavements remain almost as littered during the day. It is evident that thousands of people either lack the energy or the need, being unemployed or unemployable, to move from their gutterside homes.

'Many, clad in filthy rags or nearly naked, loll about obviously starving or half-dead. In the city centre scores of lepers and cruelly mutilated unfortunates beg unheeded . . . Roadside stalls sell food openly exposed to dust and flies which carry cholera germs. Huge garbage dumps remain uncleared and pavements are strewn with rotting trash. The gutters are the public lavatories. Dead and dying dogs as well as humans lie about the footway ... In the suburbs, conditions are far worse, with hundreds of thousands crammed into disease-breeding bustees, hutments built in foetid areas which lack sewage or running water ... Diseases like cholera and plague are endemic. Malaria, once nearly contained, is spreading again due to failure to spray mosquito-breeding swamps. Tap water is unsafe to drink and often runs black ... Trams built for 75 people carry 200 and hundreds daily risk their lives by hanging on to the footboards of overloaded buses.'

All this and more I saw in 1945. More? Trains loaded with desperate, yelling, shrieking human cargo, every inch of roof thick with bodies, every grippable piece of rolling stock precariously clutched by a desperate figure; women crawling on hands and knees along railway tracks, pathetically searching for a few walnuts of dropped coal; in the huge central market, a vast cornucopia of limes, oranges, bananas yellow and red, papayas, guavas, persimmons, pineapples, water-melons, tomatoes, grapes and indeed every kind of fruit and vegetable, tropical and temperate alike, fat rats sit with lascivious boldness among the piles of fruit while stall-holders merely laugh at them; the eternal stinking dead cow being stripped by vultures on the roadside, the eternal bloated human body floating down the Hooghli; and every morning, or almost every morning, the

sickening report in the newspapers of some young infertile Indian bride being given a can of petrol by her mother-in-law and being told that she knew what she could do with it: another human torch mercifully released from the indignity, the unforgivable sin, of not being productive, as if India's sorrowful sordid millions were not already enough.

By now it was March and India's heat was already comparable to that of a furnace; only in the first couple of hours after breakfast, in some shaded corner at the swimming pool, did I ever feel cool and fit to work. It was therefore with great relief that I met yet another of Calcutta's many Scotsmen, a tea-planter but also a public servant of integrity, a member of the Bengal Assembly, who was kind enough to invite me to spend a week-end on his estate, far to the north, within sight of the Himalayas and the foothills of Bhutan.

Before this visit could be arranged, however, he invited me to do something else: to attend a session of the Bengal Assembly. I duly went and was duly shocked. In revolting contrast to the starving, mutilated and miserable populace on the streets outside the Indian members of the Assembly were fat, oily and well-fed. They were also callous; never, in fact, had I seen the mark of evil and corruption so indelibly bitten into so many human faces at one time. Only the face of my Scottish friend and a few other specimens of the hated British Raj stood out with incorruptible integrity, like good deeds in a very naughty world.

A few days later we entrained for the north, I not having the remotest notion of what other side of India would greet me there.

VII

The scene at the railway station, on the evening of our departure, was exactly as I have already described: crowds of near-hysterical Indian bodies covering the platforms, smothering like clusters of white-winged moths the roofs and buffers and running boards of trains; an almost riotous assembly and altogether a certain air of disordered and almost childish madness. Of all this, however, my friend and I were not obliged to become part. Our first-class compartment was not only reserved but reserved for us alone. Our bearer attended to our baggage, at the same time loading into the compartment vast hampers of food and drink and other comforts.

The railway going northward through Bengal finally ends at Darjeeling, but our destination was some way to the south of the Sikkim border, at a place called Jalpagur. It was, as I remember it, only an hour or so after dawn when we arrived there, in a morning of exquisite freshness totally free of Calcutta's oppressive, sweaty humidity. So far north we could, anyway, be sure that the sun would, at that time of year, never have the implacable power it had in the south. The country air was in fact delicious; the distances were hazy, so that the peaks of the Himalayas were wholly hidden, but the foothills of Bhutan, looking strangely mysterious, brooded almost colourlessly against the northern sky.

We washed, shaved, changed and breakfasted at a club house. Smart army officers, some Indian, were breakfasting too, many of them, as I guessed, going on leave to Darjeeling. On the station platform I had already seen several people clearly coming back from Darjeeling and very refreshing it was to see two young English nurses carrying little baskets made of slender strips of wood and planted with roots of the common primrose in cool, lovely and happy flower.

After breakfast we got into my friend's waiting truck and

85

began to head eastwards, under the foothills. A considerable number of streams flow down here from the great Himalayan range and at that season of the year many of them were totally dry, mere beds of white sun-scalded rock. We crossed these by wooden bridges which, in the eventual monsoon season, would be swept away by torrents of flood water of prodigious power and would in due course have to be built up again.

But at one point we reached a river of considerable size, far too wide to be bridged, and over this we ferried the truck on a precarious arrangement of planks and petrol drums which had to be powerfully handled by numbers of natives with oars and poles in order that it didn't drift helplessly downstream. My recollection is that the men sang loud and vigorous chants, as Indians so often do when doing a job in concert, as they punted and rowed, all looking, in contrast to the miserable bags of bones in Calcutta's foetid streets, as happy as sand-boys enjoying some huge lark.

From the far river bank we eventually bowled and bumped along in a cloud of white dust which gave the impression of rising and sweeping away to the north, there to blanket the foothills in deep haze. This haze however was not of dust but already, in mid-morning, of heat. Not that the day had lost its freshness; on the contrary it had a certain spring-like air, an impression that was much strengthened when we reached my friend's tea estate and bungalow, in the garden of which sweetpeas, marigolds, petunias, sweet williams, stocks and phlox Drummondii were all in delicious flower. In the tea gardens little Indian children were picking some predatory orange-coloured bug off the camellia-like bushes, a task for which they would be paid a few annas a dozen, and occasionally an enormous and brilliant butterfly, more like bird than insect, would fly over with captivating splendour.

The bungalow itself was beautifully furnished, complete with billiard table, its furniture polished to perfection. Bare-footed Indian servants glided about everywhere, silently, and soon ice was clinking away in long glasses of gin, tonic water and green moons of lime. It was all very comfortable, very affluent, very respectable and very orderly: yet I gained an uneasy impression. It was that my friend lived a life of great loneliness. He lacked for nothing; a clap of the hands, the tinkle of a bell, would instantly bring him all he wanted, and yet the house was, it seemed to me, haunted by a great emptiness. Some few years later I put all this into a story called *The Frontier*, but even today I cannot totally rid myself of that atmosphere of empty loneliness, any more than I can expunge from my mind the heat-haze on the foothills, the giant and splendid butterflies or the little Indian children collecting their bright bugs from the bushes of tea.

That afternoon, being Saturday, my friend set off to the estate offices to pay his workers, including the little Indian children who sat outside, cross-legged, with their orange captures of bugs neatly laid out before them in the dust. My friend didn't claim that his was an exclusive or even very good brand of tea, certainly nothing resembling the nectars of Darjeeling; it was his job to produce a tea that would make 'the good strong cup' so beloved of many Britishers, whether the housewife struggling with her cooking and her washing or the truck-driver at the 'good pull-up for car-men'. But what he also produced, and which in turn I found fascinating, was a brand of brick tea made especially for Tibetans. This was compressed and solidified into black blocks the shape of thick saucers, some five inches across; they were immensely hard and heavy and would, if thrown at a man from short range, have inflicted no little injury. The interesting thing about these iron-like shapes of brick tea was that they were used by the Tibetans not only for brewing tea on long treks in wild mountain country (the tea was not only heavy and durable but almost indestructible) but also as a form of currency. My friend kindly gave me one of these formidable slabs but I must confess that I never put it to the test of boiling water.

Next morning, Sunday, we toured the estate and its environs by car. The air was again delicious, the scent of flowers in the garden tenderly exotic, as in some perfect warm English May.

Again too the foothills were shrouded in heat haze, the Himalayas completely hidden behind them. And now and then, as we drove through narrow jungle roads, the high dry elephant grass on both sides tunnelled by cavernous paths made by rhinoceros, we occasionally passed little groups of trotting Indian men, near-naked and very dark in colour, their bows and arrows slung across their shining backs as they set forth to hunt and kill something for the Sunday pot. They looked totally innocent, totally primitive, totally unsullied by what we are pleased to call civilisation. I found them most attractive and touching.

When we left a couple of days later to entrain for Calcutta I felt no little sense of regret; I would like to have seen more of the foothills, the jungle and its birds, the rivers and the dark trotting little men. Yet I was more than glad to have seen what I had seen and to know that there is a side of India that is lovable and in its own special way as unforgettable as the 'world's greatest urban disaster'. It is in fact not far from the truth to say that for a good twenty years after that visit to the hills and the tea plantation there were few days when I did not think of them and always with affection; and I think of them still.

Perhaps my pleasure at that week-end was the greater because I knew that the road to Calcutta also meant once again the road to Burma, and I have to confess that it was a journey I did not, at that moment, relish very much.

As it turned out it resolved itself more happily.

VIII

Never a lover of Kipling, I have often been puzzled by his
lines 'on the road to Mandalay, where the flying fishes play'.
It has always seemed to me odd that there should be flying
fishes at a Burmese town many hundreds of miles inland from
the sea but perhaps, since Mandalay is on the great Irrawaddy,
Kipling may have been right after all. It was not, however, to
Mandalay that I was going on my second trip to Burma, since
the town was still in Japanese hands, but to Monywa, once a
pleasant little country town but now a pathetic heap of
ruins and overgrown jungle and also on the Irrawaddy.

It was now almost April and as I stepped from the aircraft
on to the dusty airstrip the sun once again hit me a vicious,
white-hot blow. As quickly as possible I hitched a lift in a jeep,
piled my kit into the vehicle and drove off to the R.A.F. camp
on the edge of the ruined town. At the encampment I left my
belongings on the roadside, leaving a little book of Elizabethan
lyrics, bound in white vellum, on the top of them, and then went
off to find the camp adjutant and if possible a tent and a bed.
The adjutant, when found, was helpful but not hopeful. It
might mean, he explained, that I would have to share a tent with
at least one other officer if not two. I thanked him and he duly
took me off to find the tent. It then turned out that only one
other officer was in occupation, although not at home at that
moment, and I immediately went off to collect my baggage.
When I got back to it the little book of Elizabethan lyrics
presented an amazing sight. The furious heat of the sun, in
only a quarter of an hour or so, had had such a powerful
effect on the vellum that both covers were completely and
tightly curled up, like a brace of white brandy-snaps.

I had scarcely begun to unpack a few things in the tent than
my fellow tent-sharer, as if already warned by the swiftest
possible message, arrived in a state of what I think is best

described as possessive agitation. One of those born fuss-pots with an inordinate passion for tidiness, he was clearly scared stiff that I, the new intruder, would besmirch the sacred precincts of his ordered world.

I, wanting only to be friendly, showed him the strangely transformed book of Elizabethan lyrics, adding something about 'this God-awful heat', in which I was sweating ferociously.

'Heat, old boy? You don't call *this* heat, do you? I mean this is the cool season, the winter. Wait till it really warms up, say June and July – no, old boy, don't put your stuff there if you don't mind. There isn't an awful lot of room for two and I'd rather you didn't clutter things up.'

No tent in the whole of Burma could have looked less cluttered up. My companion, fussy, belly-aching, slightly effeminate, finicky of eye, had carefully seen to that. He had also carefully seen to it that every precautionary bottle of

pills, tablets, powders and so on was laid out on his bedside bamboo table in neat order ready to do battle with malaria, the common cold, heat sickness, diarrhoea, lack of salt and all the other ills which a tropical climate may, or may not, inflict on a man.

'I hope you brought your mepacrine, old boy? Terribly important. You need the proper dosage every day. I never miss.'

'Mepacrine? What's it for?'

'Good grief, old boy, you don't know? Malaria, of course. You must take it. Absolutely essential. There are chaps out here who've had malaria a dozen times, even twenty. Might never have happened if they'd been regular with the mepacrine. No, old boy, do you mind not putting your tooth brush into that beaker? It's sort of my preserve, that one.'

Hot though it was, I went outside for air. The hope that I should find it was a vain one, but I felt that if I didn't get out of that tent at once I should suddenly scream. There is no type more liable to drive me crazy than the slightly effeminate male fuss-pot, especially when the power behind it is the orderly mind. It produces in me a violent sense of impotent frustration.

Another five minutes of 'don't put your stuff there, old boy, do you mind?' and injunctions such as 'it's only fair to both of us, old boy, not to clutter the place up. There's hardly enough room for one as it is, I mean' – once again drove me out of the tent, this time in search of the Mess and a possible cup of tea. This, I thought, might at least refresh my frustrated spirit but to my infinite revulsion all I got from a diminutive Burmese bearer was a cup of what must be the world's most revolting liquid, namely tea made in the pot with sugar, condensed milk and all, the whole looking like pale liquid toffee.

Eventually I splashed about in two inches of water in my canvas field-bath, put on a clean dry shirt, my bush shirt, and a pair of slacks and then went back, in the twilight, to see if the Mess could provide anything stronger than toffee tea.

Fortifying myself with gin, I found myself being addressed by the camp Padre. This too depressed me. My long standing dislike of things parsonic at once put my back up. This, as I presently realized, was another mistake, since the Padre turned out to be neither patronising nor hearty, neither pompous nor obsequious, neither saintly nor, as I had once discovered in another Padre in another Mess, a drunk.

'Are you here for long?' he wanted to know. 'What's your particular field, if you don't mind my asking?'

I told him, explaining about the pieces I had to do for America.

91

'Very interesting. Perhaps I can help in some way.'

I thanked him and he suddenly said:

'I tell you what. I'm driving out to a Burmese village tomorrow morning. Christian community. Methodists. Care to come? You might find it interesting. We're going to choose the hymns for Easter Sunday.'

'April the first, isn't it?' I said, but he had character enough to ignore the intended joke. 'Well, it's very kind of you. I'll see what it's like in the morning.'

'I can tell you what it'll be like in the morning. Pretty damned hot. Anyway come by all means if you feel like it. I'll come and look you up after breakfast.'

That night I lay awake listening to what must be the world's most grievous, dismal, haunting sound: the wailing of a pack of jackals. The sound is like that of a crowd of imprisoned human souls suffering all the tortures of the damned, wailing in unappeasable misery, in the depths of hell.

The Padre called for me next morning, in his jeep, about ten o'clock.

'Oh! you've decided to come, have you? Good show. I think you'll find it interesting. They've some astonishing stories to tell, some of these Burmese. Pretty hair-raising too, a lot of them.'

We set off across the wide, empty, dusty, sun-scalded plain. A single-track railway, long since disused, went across it at one point, the red rusting rails ghostly in the burning sun.

I suppose we might have driven for an hour or so across the plain, on which a few white egrets looked like ghosts too, and then at length an oasis of palms, peepul trees, giant bamboos and palm-thatched huts appeared in the yellow glare ahead.

'This is our village,' the Padre said and a minute or two later we were mercifully enveloped in tree shade.

Almost at once there sprang out of the bamboos a shrieking chorus of children's voices, followed by the children themselves, their brown Asiatic faces grinning from ear to ear with explosive delight. How many of them clambered on to the jeep I simply couldn't count. Those who couldn't clamber dropped in the dust, then picked themselves up and, laughing hilariously at the enormity of the joke, ran on behind.

We finally drew up at a compound surrounded by low, palm-thatched houses having shaded verandahs decorated with a few pots of creepers and flowers. Children flopped on their bottoms in the dust as the jeep drew up sharply and the air was joyous with shrieking. This chorus of sound brought three or four Burmese women from one of the houses to shake hands, joyous themselves, with the Padre.

In turn he introduced me to the women, whose reaction was one of polite, sometimes smiling, but mostly grave shyness. Soon we were sitting on the verandah, there to be served with what was, in the rising heat of the morning, absolute nectar: long glasses of fresh lime juice, miraculously cold.

I had been happily sipping at this for perhaps five minutes when I became aware of a vision. A Burmese girl of extraordinary pale skin and very black hair and eyes, her oval face very grave, shy and statuesque, had suddenly glided silently from the house to be among us. She was wearing the simplest of white blouses and a purple wrap-over skirt. She looked every inch a dignified, beautiful, aristocratic goddess.

'This is Dorothy,' the Padre said. 'Dorothy is from the University of Rangoon, or rather she was. But she'll go back there one day, won't you, Dorothy?'

'I shall go back,' she said.

Something about the finality and certainty of these words,

93

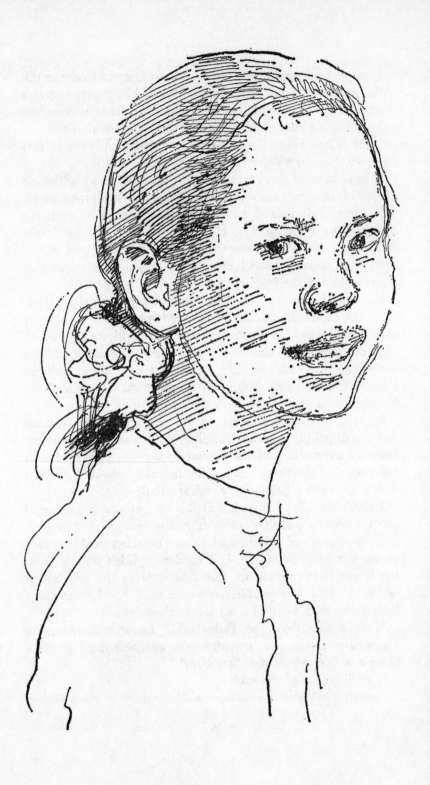

spoken in quiet perfect English, was very touching. I did not then know that she, together with the other women and many hundreds of other Burmese, had undergone a journey of sheer Hell as they trekked north for hundreds of miles in their escape from Rangoon and the pursuing Japs; nor was there any way of guessing it from that grave and exquisite young face, marvellously full of repose.

Presently, as she refilled my glass with lime-juice, the Padre said to me:

'I suppose you're not interested in jewels, are you? Almost all these villagers have stones to sell. Rubies, emeralds, amethysts, zircons, all sorts of things. Some are the genuine thing, some are what they call reconstituted, I think. You have to be careful. But if you'd care to see some Dorothy would take you to one of the houses where you'd get a fair deal.'

I confess I am not very interested in precious stones but out of politeness I said that I should like to see some. Dorothy at once put down the jug of lime-juice.

'Very well, I will take you. The house is not far.'

Dorothy and I left the verandah and walked round the compound until we came at last to another house, lived in by a rather elderly Burmese couple, and went in. What struck me at once about the interior of this house was its air of intense, provincial, almost Victorian respectability. It reminded me of the half-sacred front-room parlours of my boyhood: neat antimacassars on chairs, useless trinkets, admonishing Christian texts on the walls, a portrait of the King and Queen of England.

Presently the two Burmese were showing us a few, very small precious stones: rubies, an emerald or two, some amethysts, some sherry-gold zircons, laying them out on neat white cloths on little trays. I wasn't greatly impressed, or even greatly interested, and presently Dorothy, sensing this, began to make polite apologies for us, so that we might say good-bye.

Outside the house she gave me a quick, grave smile.

'I think the stones were not very good. You didn't want to buy?'

'No. I am sorry. I think they were not very good.'

95

'The pity is that so many bad ones are sold. The English boys buy them as souvenirs to take home without troubling even to find out if they are genuine or not. It gives us a bad name.'

'You haven't a bad name as far as I am concerned.'

'Thank you. That was very kind of you.'

We walked back to the house of Dorothy's sister. There we talked again, drank more lime-juice, and the Padre discussed the hymns for Easter Sunday. My recollection is that I talked little but listened much. 'Little pigs have big ears,' I could hear my grandmother saying and certainly, on that hot April morning I sat listening very much as I used to sit listening on cool rainy days far back in England, in the tool-shed, the hay-barn or under the cart-house, listening to my grandfather and his cronies talking politics, cursing governments, arguing, swapping stories, scandal and 'remembrance of things past'. Now, as then, I was the picker-up of unconsidered trifles, scraps of what may well have seemed to the Padre and Dorothy and the other Burmese trivialities of little or no importance but which I hid away, like precious stones themselves, in the recesses of my mind. I cannot now remember if I made any suggestions as to Easter hymns, but it is possible; my long arduous Sunday School training would certainly have stood me in good stead, since even today I can, if necessary, reel off the lines of countless hymns without ever a glance at a hymnal. But it was really not hymns that were in my mind that morning; it was largely the long trek of Burmese going northward from Rangoon and the grave dignified beauty, the courageous calm and the exquisite pallor of the young Dorothy's face.

Readers of *The Purple Plain* will not need to be told, I think, that the incidents recorded above are part of the early fabric of that novel: the drive across the scalding plain, the laughing Burmese children crowding on the jeep, the little Burmese house, the lime-juice, Dorothy and her sister, the talk, the precious stones. They will know that in the book the Padre becomes a doctor, that my fuss-pot tent-sharer becomes Blore, that Dorothy becomes Anna, that my place is taken by Forrester, a shattered R.A.F. pilot whose only wish is to die. The little ideas and pictures I gathered up that morning, the unconsidered trifles, were the genesis of the book.

But ideas alone, as I have frequently pointed out before, are of themselves not enough. The single idea that at first seems so good is more often than not sterile; it is a negative needing a positive to fire it into life – or, if you prefer it, an ovary needing to be fertilised before it can produce a living offspring. So, though the incidents and pictures of that morning were pictorially vivid and exciting enough, the truly vital part of it all, the positive agent of fertilisation, was still missing. Nor was I to find it, and then quite by accident, until I got back to the cooler, calmer pastures of England.

IX

I left Calcutta by flying-boat, for England, a week later, on April 8th. It is, I think, important to record here what the feeling in both India and Burma was, at that time, about the future of the Burma campaign. It was a bog of pessimism, a hundred miles deep. Not a soul, I think, doubted that the war would last a good ten years longer. Worse than this, and the pessimism it engendered, was an evident sickness of morale. In the Mess tent at Monywa I had heard officers, to my incredulous astonishment, openly talking what I could only tell myself was pure sedition; they were luridly blasphemous about government, higher command, the long futility of the war itself, above all the fact that the people fighting that war seemed to have been brutally forgotten. They were probably saying no more than the German infantryman said in *All Quiet on the Western Front*, what Sassoon and Graves said in *The Memoirs of an Infantry Officer* and *Good-bye to all that*, what Wilfred Owen exposed in his poems or what a million soldiers had said or thought in the holocausts of Passchendaele, Ypres, the Somme, Hill Sixty and Verdun, but its effect on me was nevertheless shattering.

This bitterness, the age-old bitterness of the deluded fighting man cursing war's futilities and politicians' duplicities, seemed finally to crystallize in my mind as the big Sunderland flying-boat flew westwards over the Hooghli River and the great scarlet steel span of the Willingdon bridge and set course for Karachi over India's deserts, rivers and palms. It crystallized; and then I put it, like some evil thought by which I didn't want to be haunted, aside. Burma, in all its vividness never to be forgotten, suddenly seemed part of an unreal past. Now I was merely glad, indeed near-exultant, to be going home.

The old Sunderland flying-boat was a huge comfortable

99

vehicle and that morning there were men and officers of all ranks, many time-expired, on board. There were also wives and children, the children running noisily about the spacious cabin decks, shouting and playing games as in a nursery at home. Officers were segregated by rank, the top brass enjoying the most superior of the boat's comforts, the rank and file herded in the tail. Thanks to this arrangement I found myself sitting next to, and finally making friends with, a young army colonel, a campaign veteran of twenty-five with five years' service in the East, a good example of the swiftness that war offers in the field of promotion. I can best describe him, I think, as the utter antithesis of my tent-sharer at Monywa, the belly-aching fuss-pot, Blore. His character was writ large, the character of a man of action, of a good talker, a good soldier, a lover of life, a bender if not breaker of rules. I liked him very much and we spent a good deal of time together, both in the air and on the ground, on the long journey home. Five years' campaigning had caused him to collect a vast amount of gear, including an enormous amount of tobacco, of which more later. This accumulated tonnage of his made my own modest suit-case, bed-roll and huge stick of still green bananas seem pathetically small. (My younger children had never even seen a banana and I was carrying home that precious green loot – of exactly the same green as the flocks of small shy parrots that I describe in *The Purple Plain* – as something infinitely more precious than all the rubies in Burma.)

In Karachi swallows were nesting under the roofs of houses and even flying about the high open-eaved rooms of our hotel. The town was not unpleasant and the people, so far as one could gather in so short a time, seemed far removed from Bengal, that 'low-lying country occupied by a low-lying people'. It was another side of India I would much like to have seen more of, but next morning we were flying on to Bahrein, a narrow-gutted town of mean, narrow streets, much dust and wind, miserable-looking Arabs huddled in what seemed to be white winding sheets, and perfectly hideous food.

This, however, only prepared us the better for Cairo, to

which we flew on next day, the flying-boat splashing down in brilliant sunshine on the Nile in a great spume of spray among the white scimitar sails of a crowd of Arab dhows. Here again was Mr Groppi's renowned *confiserie*, an El Dorado of cakes, *pâtisseries*, and every kind of sweetmeat from chocolate beans to Turkish delight. The girls behind the counters were, however, less sweet than the sweets and it wasn't until the colonel and I tried French on them that we got from them the glimmer of a smile. In the evening Cairo glowed in all its incredible brilliance, the chickens turned sizzling on their spits, and the wine glowed in our veins.

We flew on next day to the tip of Sicily, to Augusta, and another dose of contrasts. Unlike Cairo, Italy had not had a cosy war; and though Augusta's streets were brilliant with mimosa and many cherry-red geraniums the air seemed to me dark with blight. As we sat in a *café* drinking some impossible concoction or other I became aware of a low scurrying, as of mice, at the foot of the doorway. This, we discovered, was the work of three or four ragged Sicilian urchins, fishing for cigarette butts from the floor of the *café*, their rod and line being a length of wire twisted into a ring at one end, the ring finally hooking the cigarette end and dragging it under the door. The desperate poverty of all this was repeated in doorways and on doorsteps in the streets outside, where mothers were offering their own and their daughters' beds and bodies to all who cared to pay and pick. It was a moment of degradation that I found more sickening even than Calcutta's rancid iniquities.

Next day we flew into Poole Harbour on an afternoon of such exquisite warm brilliance that it might well have been that we had packaged the weather in Cairo and brought it home. An Egyptian on the plane, clearly all-prepared for England's notorious and traditional gloom and fog, simply sat staring in stunned disbelief at a sky that in its deep azure made even Cairo's look pallid by comparison. I confess I could hardly believe it myself and I underwent a small earthquake of emotion.

Continually, on that last section of the flight, my young colonel friend had held discourse on the delicate question of H.M. Customs and Excise and the equally delicate question of 'knowing the ropes'.

'It's a cinch, old boy. Leave it all to me. I've got the whole ruddy thing taped.'

'You've got rather a lot of tobacco, you said. What about that?'

'Piece o' cake. Nothing to it, old boy. Leave it to me. Had all the gen in a letter from a type who flew home a couple of weeks ago. Loaded with jewels, rugs, silks, tobacco and all the riches of Samarkand and all that and just sailed through like an innocent. Never touched him for a farthing. It's all a question, old boy, of knowing the ropes.'

We were eventually called to the customs' desks in order of rank, so that my colonel friend preceded me, going to a room upstairs. 'Back in a jiff, old boy,' he called and waved a cheery hand. The jiff became ten minutes, then twenty. At this stage I was called for customs' examination and duly declared various bits of silk and clothing and chocolate and sweets, but no tobacco. The duty turned out to be trivial and I was cleared in, I should say, five minutes. At the end of it I looked and waited, in vain, for my friend. His jiff became half an hour, then three quarters. Then slowly a shattered figure came downstairs, pale and haggard, all confidence drained away. Positively groping his way towards me across the customs' hall, he finally halted, shaking his head.

'Wanted thirty-five quid for the tobacco alone, old boy. Sixty-five for the lot. I just hadn't got it. Had to leave the whole bloody lot in bond.'

Fortunately he was able to drown his sorrows on the train. There, to our infinite astonishment, we found a Pullman car – the only Pullman car, as I understood it, still running in war-time England. Several times on the flying-boat journey my colonel friend had wagged his head sagely at me and declared that we were, in his opinion, a couple of ripe old bastards. Now it was obvious that we were a pair of kings, wining and

dining at the Ritz. We luxuriated; the steward found us a bottle
of wine and even, I think, some brandy.

Thus bathed in refreshment and contentment I gazed out
on England, my beloved England. Never, I kept telling myself,
had it looked so beautiful. Green meadows, woods rich with
golden sallow and white with 'loveliest of trees, the cherry',
gardens alight with daffodils and tulips and even, so early in
the year, lilacs in pink and white blossom. This was my own, I

kept telling myself, my native land, and unashamedly let
my eyes fill with tears, so that the countryside slipping by the
train windows in the golden glory of evening light became a
trembling evanescence of green and blue and gold.

It was late when I arrived home in a night as balmy as in
a perfect July. The air was sweet breath on my face, the garden

full of scent. I gazed for a few moments on a luxuriant bed of polyanthus that seemed like the very epitome of all that was loveliest in an English spring, then gathered my suit-case, my bed-roll and my bananas from my car.

The kitchen door was unlocked. I dumped my stuff by the stove, then tip-toed upstairs and folded a wakeful Madge in my arms.

X

Old and worn though such clichés as 'living in a dream' and 'walking on air' undoubtedly are, there are times, I think, when even they are permissible. Certain it is that for the next few days, even the next few weeks, I felt myself to be living in a dream, walking on air. Both the dream and the air, of purest April Englishness, were as sweet as spring water after the drought of a desert. I couldn't drink enough of them.

The weather in that still taut-stretched brittle April of 1945 continued to be miraculous. Every day the temperatures, steadily in the eighties, were more like July than April. Dudley Barker, glad to see me back again, I think, and pleased enough with the pieces I had written, generously gave me leave and day after day Madge and I took the children to the sea. The sense of liberation was also miraculous; so that I couldn't have cared a tinker's cuss whether the war ended or not. Certainly, in Europe, it looked like ending, but such hopes had risen before, only for the resilience of the Germans to put us again in jeopardy.

But soon, on a day when the world was half-jubilant, half-ashamed, the first atomic bomb was dropped on Hiroshima and the apparently endless war in Burma was incredibly over, as the war in Europe already was. After that stupendous event a great sense of pointlessness prevailed; an occasional visit to Air Ministry induced nothing but boredom and irritating frustration. There was nothing to do. Nor, I found, could I work at home. Indeed I frequently feared, as writers often do, that I might never write any more, that the spring waters of imagination had dried up and would never flow again. During the war I had in fact written precious little outside such writing as I had done for the R.A.F.; indeed, all I had to show for the past five years, on my own account, was *The Modern Short Story*, a critical study of the *genre* and some of its exponents, a *novella*, the first I had written but by no means the last, called *The Bride Comes to Evensford*, a few reviews and *Fair Stood the Wind For France*: hardly a rich harvest, nor a great source of revenue until *Fair Stood the Wind For France* achieved its welcome success.

Then, towards the latter part of the summer, came my papers for demobilisation. On the appointed day I drove the car up to Air Ministry, there to discover, to my joy, that R. F. Delderfield, already bursting with the phenomenal success of *Worm's Eye View*, together with some others from P.R., had forgathered for demobbing too. We all piled into my car and drove jubilantly to Uxbridge. Incredibly, when we reached the R.A.F. Station there, I found myself in the very same room that had been my dormitory on my first day in uniform, a totally unexpected completion of the circle that immediately caused the comedian in me to jump out, as R. F. Delderfield has well described in his *Overture for Beginners*:

'It had been a day for new beginnings, or so H. E. Bates declared as he pranced about the Demob Centre in his Squadron-Leader's uniform, topped by a loud coster-type

106

civvy cap, and looking as incongruous as a pantomime comedian in Ascot rig. Bates and I had been two of the first P.R. men in the game, scoring heavily on the points system that controlled demobilisation. He was forty and I was thirty-three, with five and a half years' service, so we said our farewells and trundled down the spiral staircase to the lift, schoolboys on the last day of term.'

The spiral staircase referred to was at Air Ministry, but before we reached that high point of our jubilations something of much greater significance had occurred. On the way to Uxbridge, before the fooling began, someone casually asked me if I had ever met a certain fighter pilot whose name I have long forgotten. I replied that I didn't think I ever had.

'Remarkable type. Had more gongs than anyone I ever knew. And got them all for trying to kill himself.'

I asked to be enlightened on this unusual situation and was told that the pilot had taken his bride, only a few hours after they were married, to a celebratory dance at a night club in Leicester Square. Suddenly, as they danced, a bomb scored a direct hit on the club, killing scores of people and also blowing the young bride out of the pilot's arms, killing her outright without injuring him. The grievous shock of all this was so great that when he went back to duty it was with the avowed intention of getting himself killed. Instead, by the bitterest of ironies, he merely succeeded in collecting a fabulous number of medals – and remained alive.

In a flash I realized that this was the positive I had been seeking for my Burma negative. This was the key that would wind up the spring that would set the mechanism ticking, so that Blore, the Padre, Dorothy, the Burmese girl killing the lizard, the laughing Burmese children and all the rest could come to life in new identity. My secret jubilation at this was infinitely greater than the jubilation at merely getting out of uniform, so that I could scarcely wait to get my hands on a white virgin ream of paper and begin to set down my version of the Burma scene:

'Shy flocks of small banana-green parrots had begun to come back to the peepul trees about the bombed pagoda. But across the rice-fields, scorched and barren now from the long dry season, only a few white egrets stepped daintily like ghostly cranes about the yellow dust in the heat-haze. Nothing else moved across the great plain where for three years no rice had grown.'

So for the next three months or more I was in imagination back in Burma, inventing, remembering, re-enacting scenes, incidents, people; nursing Forrester, the pilot, through his grief and cryptic bitterness, redepicting Dorothy as Anna, the salve to the pilot's unhealed wounds, the Padre as the doctor and my insufferable fuss-pot tent-sharer as Blore. Some of the white heat of Burma got into my blood as I wrote, so that the words came out as if driven by a blow-torch. The subsequent book trebled the success of *Fair Stood the Wind For France*, bringing me a vast new readership. It also became a film in which Gregory Peck was wholly admirable as Forrester ('Your damn book nearly killed me,' he told me, referring to his long foot-slog with his shot-down companions, Carrington and Blore, through Burma's pitiless heat;) with a young unknown Burmese girl from Rangoon playing Anna with all the beauty, restraint, withdrawal and gravity so necessary to the part.

Not that the book pleased everybody. Certain of my friends, whose critical acumen I highly esteem, made deep noises of disapproval. They referred me back to such books of mine as *The Poacher* and *The Fallow Land*. 'This,' they lectured me, 'is what we want from you. Not your hot, wretched Burma plain.' Useless for me to try to explain the powerful and almost catastrophic impact the East had had on my sensitivity; hopeless to try to convey the blistering effect of its fatalism, which Conrad had seen and interpreted so well, its callous contempt for life, expressed in the episode of the little girl and the lizard, or the blistering, pulverising heat; pointless to protest that this was an explosive revolution in my life that simply *had* to be set down, or that, God being my helper, I would surely return to depicting 'England's green and pleasant land', which assuredly, in due time, I did.

If I claim nothing else for myself as a writer I will not deny myself versatility. The same hand that writes *My Uncle Silas* also produces *Fair Stood the Wind For France;* the same imagination that produces the Chaucerian farces of the Larkin family is also responsible for the unremitting tragedy of *The Triple Echo;* the same brain that is responsible for *The Poacher* also produces the stories of 'Flying Officer X'. No: if I claim nothing else for myself I will certainly claim that I am versatile.

So it was that within a year or so the hand that had written *The Poacher, Uncle Silas, The Bride Comes to Evensford, The Fallow Land* and the two books into which I have perhaps best distilled my love and feeling for the English countryside, *Through the Woods* and *Down the River,* turned its attention to a second novel of Burma, *The Jacaranda Tree.* This I approached with no little trepidation. For whereas I had seen the terrain and the people of *The Purple Plain* and had absorbed the electrifying atmosphere of central Burma through not only my eyes but the very pores of my skin, I had seen not one inch of the far distant territory over which the long and tragic trek to India had been made in bitter and horrifying circumstances when the Japanese had occupied Singapore and invaded Burma in 1942. I could only imagine what it could be like. But, I asked myself, was imagination enough? Could I possibly re-create the journey that had caused the planter in the Hendersons' flat in Calcutta such alcoholic remorse, and its terrain and atmosphere? I had asked myself very much the same question before writing *Fair Stood the Wind For France.* In that case too I had seen no more than a fraction of the terrain; I was largely unfamiliar with French provincial life even in peace-time let alone in that of war; all, or mostly all, had to be invented. Now I could only hope that, since the earlier novel had achieved the necessary authenticity, my imagination and instinct would again carry me towards the heart of the truth.

The surrender of Singapore and the invasion of Burma by the

Japanese were two inglorious moments in British imperial history, though certainly no more inglorious than the cataclysm that overtook America at Pearl Harbor, an event which, in my experience, few Americans to this very day care to discuss. Nor were they as great a humiliation as the fall of France in 1940; but let us say that they were in all conscience grim enough. Thus when I came to write *The Jacaranda Tree* I felt I could not, so to speak, overdo its agony. Through the experiences of Patterson, the planter, his boy Tuesday, and other characters, I told myself that, sparing nothing, I must re-create that agony. Again, to this end, as in *The Purple Plain*, I wrote in white-hot heat.

Some few years later I met a lady who asked me, quite simply:

'Were you on the retreat from Burma?'

'No,' I confessed, 'I was not.'

'But I feel you must have been.'

A great foreboding suddenly took hold of me. Had I painted the scene in *The Jacaranda Tree* well or falsely? Had I over-painted it or not?

'You mean,' I said, 'that I have – '

'My sister and I,' she said, 'were in that retreat. If you had exaggerated ten times over what you wrote you would still have been a hundred miles short of the truth. It was truly more ghastly than you could possibly imagine.'

When the book finally appeared it achieved an even greater sale than *The Purple Plain*, again greatly enlarging my readership. But again there were also dissentient voices from friends whose critical judgement I had learned to respect. Yet again it was useless to point out the compulsion of all the circumstances that lay behind the book – the East's unforgettable vividness of scene, the catastrophic nature of the retreat itself, the fatalism, the relentless heat, the provincial pettiness of colonial types such as the Portmans and the devotion to duty and causes as exemplified by Major Brain. Nor would it have profited me to point out that I was by no means the first European, whether writer or painter, to have been so fascinated and seduced by the East as to turn his back on Europe, if only temporarily. Maugham, the young doctor of *Liza of Lambeth*, had found himself under a comparable compulsion to write of Malaya; D. H. Lawrence, brought up on pit-baths in front of kitchen fires in Nottinghamshire, had found himself similarly compelled by Mexico; Gauguin, seemingly content enough to portray the lace-capped peasants of Pont Aven and surrounding Brittany, had suddenly abandoned it all to paint the languorous naked ladies so free with their charms far away in Tahiti.

Nor was it at any time my intention to make my severance with English ties anything but temporary. 'He's finished!' one of these friends cried as he wholeheartedly fell on the two Burma novels, little realizing that in many ways the best in me was yet to be, as he himself later readily admitted. Apart from the fact that it was surely singularly unjust to judge a writer on two books alone it was also singularly silly, in my view, not to recognise that so great and explosive an experience as the East had afforded me could by no means be cast aside and forgotten as if it were some trivial summer tea party. The effect of my visit to India and Burma, brief though it may have been, had been almost to give me a disease. Its toxins had somehow to be got out of my system or paralyse me for ever, and writing about it all was, as I saw it, the only cure.

If I had ever felt any conscious compulsion to rehabilitate myself with these dissentient friends – and I certainly never did – I could have pointed to another war-book of mine, *The Cruise of the Breadwinner*, which the critic James Agate was good enough, to my intense satisfaction, to compare with Conrad's *Typhoon*. This, the second *novella* I had attempted, was a sea-story that I readily admit had drawn some of its inspiration from Stephen Crane's *Red Badge of Courage*, surely the prime example of the triumph of imagination over observation, for the simple reason that Crane hadn't even been born when the American Civil War of which he wrote with such cauterising brilliance and realism was being fought – a realism and brilliance that had caused ecstatic English critics to compare the young American with Zola and Tolstoy. Truly imagination had carried Crane nearer to the heart of truth than observation could ever have done.

The theme of my long-short story was not wholly dissimilar to his. Whereas his starry-eyed hero goes out, as so many before and after him have done, to seek the glory of war on battle-fields, only to suffer the cruellest disillusionment, my similarly starry-eyed hero is a mere boy who goes out to sea in a rickety fishing boat, manned only by a fat skipper and a jaundiced engineer and armed only with an impossibly absurd Lewis gun, to seek his glory and to find his particular disillusionment in the lamplight of the little cabin of the vessel, in a darkening afternoon in the English Channel, as he watches two pilots, one English, one German, die together, indistinguishable in death as enemy or friend but merely representative 'of all the pilots, all the dead pilots, all over the world . . . And there rose up in him a grave exultation. He had been out with men to War and had seen the dead. He was alive and *The Breadwinner* had come home.'

The little story is certainly one of which I am not ashamed and perhaps this is as good a place as any in which to discourse briefly on the fascination the *novella* has long had for me. I was first drawn to it through Conrad, whose *Youth*, *Heart of Darkness* and other essays in the form are in classical mould. These had had the greatest possible effect on me in my youth. Later came Tolstoy, with the incomparable *Death of Ivan Ilyitch*, the grave beauty of *Family Happiness* and others. Side by side with them I read such pieces as Tchehov's *The Party*, Maupassant's *Boule de Suif*, James Joyce's *The Dead* and later Hemingway's *The Snows of Kilimanjaro*, Sherwood Anderson's *The Triumph of the Egg* and Katherine Anne Porter's *Noon Wine*. These all caused me to reflect what a marvellous achievement it is to pack into a hundred pages what many another writer would spin out diffusely into five hundred and in doing so perhaps achieve an even greater and more memorable impact.

To reach this difficult and desirable end requires, without doubt, great technical skill. 'The *novella*,' a critic wrote recently, 'is a form of notorious difficulty. It must combine the shock or finality of the short story with the psychological complication and density of medium available to the novel.' This is well said; but what is highly astonishing is not how few but how many writers of recent times have been eager to accept the challenge, to the singular enrichment of modern literature. Pushkin, Poe, Tchehov, Maupassant, Kipling, Maugham, Mann, Bunin, Crane, Wells, James, Sherwood Anderson, Knut Hamsen, Hemingway, Conrad, Thornton Wilder, Katherine Anne Porter, Graham Greene, D. H. Lawrence, Oscar Wilde, Joyce – the list of brilliant exponents in the form is as rich as it is seemingly endless.

I now resolved, therefore, to try to add to it myself. The challenge having been taken up I presently produced a volume of four *novellas* called *The Nature of Love*, only to be warned by my publishers that 'of course it won't sell. You must resign yourself to that.' In fact it did sell and indeed so well that I have ever since been more and more attracted to the form, so that I have now written some twenty *novellas*, the most recent being *The Triple Echo*, itself a supreme example of the form's 'notorious difficulty'.

The Triple Echo in fact took precisely twenty-five years to write, its genesis having begun in the darker days of the war, in 1943, its completion coming in 1968 – shades of 'the path of art endlessly difficult', of which Edward Garnett had warned me long ago in his preface to *The Two Sisters*. I will not of course mislead the reader by pretending that every day of that twenty-five years was spent in wrestling with that one particular story; it is enough to say that the challenge, the problem and the complexity were always there, constantly kicking away at the womb of the mind, the story apparently unwilling to be born but ever restless in its tireless determination finally to come to life.

Any writer of fiction will tell you that inevitably, from time to time, he finds it necessary to invent a new character to do the work of unravelling his narrative for him. In the case of *The Triple Echo* the exact reverse was true. What had so long inhibited the birth of my story was not the lack of a character but the fact that, as I belatedly discovered, I had one character too many. This superfluous character having been removed, light instantly flooded in on to a canvas that had been so long irremediably dark, and in a mere three weeks the story was extracted from the womb it had apparently been so reluctant to leave. 'The path of art endlessly difficult' indeed.

In 1947, however, *The Triple Echo* was still in the womb and it looked as if nothing less than an operation would ever get it out. Instead of which another crisis in my life occurred.

In the early spring of that year, on a visit to my parents in Northamptonshire, I became aware of a curious lassitude. My arms and legs began to feel as if made of lead; I could scarcely drag myself about. For a time I put this down to the fact that my native town, Rushden, is a town of steep hills and that since I hadn't paid a visit to the town for a considerable time I wasn't at all used to them. But as we drove back to Kent in the car, with snow falling dismally on the Downs, I felt no better. If anything the heavy lassitude seemed worse. Nor did it improve matters to discover, next morning, that my youngest son looked all set for a bout of measles. We accordingly called in the doctor.

When he arrived, however, he scarcely looked at the boy. Instead he asked what was the matter with me, at the same time looking at me seriously and very searchingly. In reply I told him of my extreme lassitude; in fact he didn't need to be told. He had already guessed what was wrong. He murmured something about samples of this and that and that he would call to collect them later. Next morning he telephoned me with the news that he had spoken with a surgeon; the fact was that I had had an internal haemorrhage and the time had come 'to take that little look inside me'.

It was now Easter Sunday, exactly two years after my trip across the Burma plain with the Padre. I do not recall that the news that I was to have an operation, and with all speed at that, in any sense depressed me; I felt rather a sense of blessed

114

relief, glad that at last there might be some chance of ridding myself of the gnawing abdominal pains, with their attendant greyness of spirit, that had troubled me ever since my teens. I therefore surrendered willingly to hospital and the surgeon next day.

The operation having been completely successful I made the swiftest possible recovery and was home again within ten days. In less than another two weeks I was in Switzerland, convalescing, carrying with me words of great assurance from the surgeon. 'Diet? Fiddlesticks. You don't suppose I've taken away seven-eighths of your stomach so that you can spend the rest of your life on a diet, do you? No, I've done what I have done for precisely the opposite reason.'

From that moment my pains vanished; the greyness of spirit was dissipated; I was a new man.

XI

A great many first novels, as I have remarked before, are autobiographical, if not wholly so then at least in part. My own first novel, *The Two Sisters*, was a marked exception. Not a single syllable of it is autobiographical; in no sense, physically, emotionally or otherwise, can the identity of any of its characters be confused with mine. It is a work, as I have also pointed out, of wild, youthful imagination: an imagination not knowing quite where it is going or what exactly it wants to say. If the result is therefore sometimes confused that is the inevitable fruit of inexperience; I felt much, imagined much but at the age of eighteen and nineteen, simply didn't know enough.

In 1950, however, at the age of forty-five, I at last began to turn my attention, for the first time, to a subject that was autobiographical. It had been many years since I had seen the figure of a strikingly beautiful young girl in a black cloak lined with scarlet arrive at the station at Rushden in a smart pony-drawn gig in order to catch a train and almost as many since, on a freezing winter night, I had gone on an assignment as a young reporter to Rushden Hall, totally unaware at the time that I was sitting in the same room in which the poet Robert Herrick must have sat, three hundred years before, on his visits to the ever-hospitable Sir Lewis Pemberton. The two incidents in fact provide another good example of a negative, in this case the unknown young girl, needing a positive, in this case the draughty Elizabethan Hall where I had sat as a nervous young reporter, in order to bring it to life.

Now, at long last, the fusion of these two episodes was complete and I began to feel life flowing from it strongly. The novel I had in mind was to reflect, in part at least, my own youth, its ecstasies and uncertainties, its impatient disposition to judge people (as I had judged my friend the Reverend Bernard Harris) by prejudice, before giving them a chance, its

love and love's attendant agonies, its inevitable disillusionments and pain and its final awakening. The theme and spirit of
Love for Lydia may perhaps be best expressed in a couple of
lines taken from the book itself: 'it had not occurred to me that
the pain of love might be part of its flowering ... With incon-
ceivable stupidity I had not given love to her simply out of fear
of being hurt by its acceptance; I had not grasped that I might
have made her suffer'.

I set this tortured piece of self-examination against my native
Nene Valley, where I had skated in winter in meadows of
frozen flood water, had wandered in spring and summer with
my grandfather, seeing the April unfolding of blackthorn and
hawthorn and king-cup and cowslip, watching kingfishers
swoop across the river and pike sunning themselves in smooth
waters, and had later so often wandered alone, trying to escape

the drabness of my native boot-and-shoe town, wrestling with
ideas for my earliest stories, unable to share with another soul
the problems they continually created. If certain of my friends
had entertained grave doubts about me after *The Purple Plain*
and *The Jacaranda Tree* they could certainly find no cause for
complaint here; all the distilled essence of the countryside I
had so loved as a boy went into *Love for Lydia*, together with the
bloom of youth, with all its beauty and tender, tenuous fragility.

Not that the completed book was achieved without much
heart-searching. A novel may be autobiographical, either

wholly or in part, but this does not at all mean that its execution is merely a question of dipping into memory and fishing out a fact here, an episode there; the birth pains of imaginative creation have still to be endured, the path of art is still endlessly difficult.

Even at the risk of my seeming to be repetitious on the subject of art's difficulties I feel this may nevertheless be a good moment to point out one of the chief sources, indeed perhaps *the* chief source, of these difficulties. It is all too often forgotten, I feel, that all art is ultimately a physical act. Art does not consist of merely dreaming dreams, of hearing the music of the spheres or, as Ibsen was fond of repeating, 'wearing vine leaves in one's hair'. As with love itself the ultimate moment of art's expression is, and must be, physical. This is not merely 'a consummation devoutly to be wished' but one which must at all costs be accomplished. Until the writer puts his pen to paper, the artist his brush or pencil to canvas or paper, the sculptor his chisel to stone or wood, until the composer gives his musicians the opportunity of making music physically possible, there is nothing. This may sound a truism; but it does much to show, I think, that while artistic creation has its own special exhilarations it can also be, and very, very often is, both physically and mentally exhausting. A great amount of self-discipline is needed to accomplish these things and this too increases the tensions and problems constantly facing the artist. Altogether it is a highly complex business and one about which, I often feel, the public knows little or nothing. Perhaps only the artist, struggling to discipline himself, seeking his tortuous way through the maze of thought and imagination and finally arriving at his final moment of exhilarating but exhausting consummation, knows exactly what price art extracts from its executors.

If my world was now achieving ripeness in many directions, some of them totally unexpected, there were still parts of its territory where this had not proved possible. One of these was the theatre. It is true that my first published book was a play, although an extremely short one, in one act, to be followed within a short time by another in one act for radio. It is also true that, nursing fond ambitions, I had as a young man read almost as voraciously of drama as I had of the short story. Ibsen, Tchehov, Turgenev, Bjornsen, Pirandello, Shakespeare, the Elizabethans, Congreve, Sheridan, Shaw, Maugham, O'Neill, Coward, O'Casey: I had swallowed them all, and more, with the keenest appetite. I sought desperately to be a dramatist. On this score Edward Garnett, never forgetting his own disastrous crash with his play *The Breaking Point*, a disaster so remorselessly predicted by Conrad, was for ever trying to turn me away from this course, but I fear I hardly listened. In consequence I wrote other one-act plays, following them up with three-acters, of which I have, I suppose, written seven or eight. Some of these have been performed and are still being performed; the larger part, though attracting the interest and even enthusiasm of an impresario here, an actor-manager there, have not.

The first of these was a piece called *Carrie and Cleopatra*, which was put on, thanks to the tireless interest of that ever-present help in time of trouble, Violet Dean, at the Torch Theatre, one of London's many little theatres of that time, just before the war. Though giving good acting scope to several of the actors, it wasn't very well received. I was not unnaturally disappointed, though undeterred. The result was that on that first memorable assignment to the R.A.F. Bomber Command Station at Oakington it was at first not in the form of short stories that I saw myself expressing the lives and actions of the young pilots there, but in a play. It so happened, however, that before the play could get itself down on paper Terence Rattigan turned up with *Flare Path*, the idea of which wasn't wholly dissimilar to the one I had in mind. I herefore put the idea of the play aside and concentrated, wisely I think, on the stories that were eventually to appear under the pseudonym of Flying Officer X. Not that the idea of the play was dead; on the contrary it continued to be agitated with life and finally became, later in the war, *The Day of Glory*.

Unhappily it proved impossible to produce it until the war was over, a fact that undoubtedly mitigated against any possible commercial success. By that time all fervour for the war had been dissipated and when at last *The Day of Glory* was produced at the Embassy Theatre one could only sense, on the first night, an atmosphere cold and disillusioned. Several parts in the play were also badly miscast, the result being that what I had wanted to say never got put over. The play fared far better on tour, under the auspices of the Arts Council, finding far better acting and far warmer audiences in the provinces than in London, where hard-bitten first night audiences often do as much to kill a play's chances of success as the hostility of critics. *The Day of Glory* is, however, still performed and has even achieved, in Holland, a state of some permanency as an annual event.

I followed this with a dark, Ibsen-like piece called *The Spider Love* (I culled the title from Donne's great lines *But O, self-traitor, I do bring The spider love, which transubstantiates all, And can convert manna to gall*) but its demands on actors are incontestably formidable and it is probably for this reason that it has never been performed. Two other plays have shared the same fate, thus emphasising, if that were necessary, the theatre's eternal uncertainty. The pains and perils of this uncertainty have been well examined and described by my former R.A.F. colleague R. F. Delderfield, who in spite of the phenomenal success of his *Worm's Eye View*, which ran for five and a half years in London, beating even the fantastic pre-war run of

Chu Chin Chow, finally turned his back on the theatre through sheer disenchantment and settled for the less maddening demands of the novel. I can only say that I wholeheartedly share both his views and his disenchantment, so that I fear the Great Bates Play will not, now, ever be written. Nor will this state of affairs break my heart; the theatre is, I realize at last, not for me.

But in the early fifties I had suffered no such disenchantment with the novel. The considerable success of *Love for Lydia* had on the contrary given me fresh heart to set at least another novel in my native Northamptonshire, in whose soil, although I had by now lived in the idyllic pastures of Kent for exactly the same time as I had lived between the valleys of the Nene and the Ouse, my roots still lay deep.

It is a commonplace in art that writers and painters – painters perhaps the more frequently – are often so fascinated by a theme, a scene or a face that they are unable to resist the temptation to do another and even perhaps yet another and another version of it. This was something of the case with the novel I now planned. As a young man, still only in my twenties, I had written my second novel, *Catherine Foster*, very much under the influence of Flaubert. Its theme concerned a woman of passionate nature and imagination married to a small-town bore who could satisfy neither her passion nor her love of music and her appetite for a warmer, freer life. Like many women before her in similar circumstances she takes a lover, enjoys a spell of excruciating happiness and then eventually goes back 'into that obscurity from which she had once come'.

Since writing that book I had had many successes along with some dismal failures brought about largely by my own obtuse stupidities; of these I have written in *The Blossoming World*. But having learned much from these failures I felt I had now matured enough, both in character and technique, to attempt a bolder version of the earlier theme. *Catherine Foster* had been set in a quiet back street of the little Northamptonshire town of Higham Ferrers, which may fairly be called my spiritual birthplace, since most of the golden days of my childhood had been spent in and about it. The new novel, *The Sleepless Moon*, was to be set just round the corner from that quiet street, in the enchanting little chestnut-lined square which to this day is virtually unchanged from the time when I used to go with my grandfather in summer to gather loads of sweet honey pears from the walled garden of a grocer's shop standing in the corner of the square, by the gates of the church. Catherine Foster had been married to a corn merchant; Constance Turner was married to a grocer in the corner shop. 'After all there were no carriages for her wedding. The distance between the church porch and the house on the corner of the square was so short, everyone said, that it was not worth while.'

It was not only carriages, however, that were missing from Constance Turner's marriage; to her bitter surprise the very essence of it was also missing, the very fact of physical love and consummation. To so sensitive a creature such a discovery is little short of tragic; she is driven more and more into herself, imprisoned in solitariness, so that soon she is known as 'the untouchable Mrs T.' Not surprisingly she, too, out of sheer desperation, takes a lover and thereby enjoys a few months of secret idyllic passion. But if the lovers' clandestine meetings are idyllic they are also pierced with pain and the novel moves to its inevitably unhappy climax as surely as any Greek tragedy.

This tragedy of incompatibility is made the more excruciating, I feel, for being set against the calm and serenity of the little town, a town of provincial conventions and gossip, of small intrigues, of church-going on Sundays and fox-hunting in winter: a town in which to such a man as Melford Turner the death of his favourite horse is a greater source of grief than the apparent frigidity of a wife on whom his 'undemonstrative, customary, nightly salutation', a kiss on the forehead, 'a mere brush of dry lips,' has an effect 'as if a great draught of wintry air had solidified inside her, gripping her heart in a freezing neutral shroud'.

All this was far removed from the heat and horrors of *The Purple Plain* and *The Jacaranda Tree;* I was now securely back on my own territory and the result, I confess, did not displease me. It therefore came as a highly discomforting shock to learn that a friend whom I constantly treated as a confidant had reputedly called the novel 'a disgusting book'. This may appear as a criticism both trivial and ludicrous in our contemporary permissive age but at the time it was solemnly and seriously meant. In turn I took it with equal solemnity and seriousness. It was not so much that I was angered; I simply felt crushed by a profound depression; my renewed confidence in myself was suddenly and completely drained away.

When Edward Garnett had lambasted the liver and lights out of me for the *débâcle* I had committed in my early ill-fated novel *The Voyagers* I had simply bounced back next day like a jack-in-the-box, eager to atone for my fatuous misdeeds. Not so with *The Sleepless Moon;* suddenly and quite illogically I was ashamed of the book. I deliberately refrained from reading any notices of it; in my heart I disowned it; and worse still I came to a stubborn and depressing decision: I would never, never write another novel.

I did not then know that David Garnett, an old friend for whose judgement I had the deepest respect, had called *The Sleepless Moon* 'a very great novel'; nor was I to know for some years later, when my vow never to write another novel had achieved an obstinate permanency. Perhaps if I had known of David's judgement at the time the course of my creative output, over the next few years, might have been charted very differently. But the fact is that I did not know and it was fortunate that my native buoyancy again came to my rescue.

The immediate result of that depressive and ill-conceived

judgement on *The Sleepless Moon* was in fact to drive me straight back into the arms of my first love, the short story, and at the same time to induce the *novella* more and more to share the bed with us. As a consequence I wrote much in both media. The discipline so necessary in the execution of the *novella*, the form of 'notorious difficulty', was not only highly challenging but highly exciting too. I have rarely enjoyed writing as much as I did in the next decade, when I produced half a dozen volumes of short stories and almost as many of *novellas*, among them such pieces as *Death of a Huntsman, An Aspidistra in Babylon, The Golden Oriole* and *Where the Cloud Breaks*, all of which I deem to belong to my best work. The judgement on *The Sleepless Moon* may perhaps be left, therefore, to the department of 'it's an ill wind'. Certainly, on reflection, I am not sorry to have been relieved, for a time at any rate, of the exhausting labours of giving birth to novels. I can only say that I greatly enjoyed, and learned much from, my repeated honeymoons with my first and second loves, the short story and the *novella*.

Moreover these numerous excursions into the shorter fictional forms merely served to prove, if proof were needed, the truth of William Gerhardi's assertion that 'fiction is the natural heir to poetry', a belief shared by Elizabeth Bowen when she claims that 'the short story is at an advantage over the novel and can claim nearer kinship to poetry, because it must be more concentrated, can be more visionary and is not weighted down (as the novel is bound to be) by facts, explanation, or analysis'. Commenting on this Lord David Cecil writes: 'she is right; just because it is as brief as a lyric poem its scope is wider; it can include the visionary and the fantastic as the novel cannot.'

In every sense, then, the aftermath of *The Sleepless Moon* was another phase in my ripening world. Inevitably it led to others, with some of which I shall now proceed to deal.

It is many years now since the short story writer A. E. Coppard first explained to me his contention that we short story writers could learn much from the cinema. I listened with

fascination to his discourse on cuts, close-ups, fade-outs and
brief swift shots and of how in this way a film was built up to
achieve a sharp, pictorial impact. In the same way, Coppard
contended, a story should be built up, achieving a comparable
visual effect. 'I want to *see* it,' Coppard said. 'I must *see* it.'
In other words the short story had to be pictorial rather than
discursive or as Miss Bowen rightly says in the passage quoted
above 'not weighted down (as the novel is bound to be) by
facts, explanation, or analysis'. I was so impressed by the
Coppard theory that I instantly resolved to make my writing
more and more visual, painting the words rather than writing
them, depicting scene and place and people vividly, in pictures,
leaving out explanations, letting only essentials do the work.
This I have done ever since, thus developing a quality that
Edward Garnett had shrewdly detected in *The Two Sisters* –
namely that 'the story is implied rather than chronicled'.

It is here worth pointing out that *The Sleepless Moon* is
dedicated to David Lean, the film director, who had learned
his craft in that graveyard of inessentials, the cutting room.
It was not to David Lean, however, that I first owed my
association with films, though he was later to buy the rights
of several of my stories for that medium. I owed my introduction to films to an American director, Leslie Fenton. It is
really wrong, however, to refer to Fenton as an American and
I do so only because he had worked solely in America, as a
director, for many years. He was in fact English, having stead-
fastly refused, like Chaplin, to give up his nationality. His
devotion to and admiration for England were indeed great,
so much so that as soon as the Second World War broke out
Fenton immediately shipped himself to England and joined
the Royal Navy. In due course he fought in that vicious engage-
ment, the Battle of St Nazaire, where he was badly wounded
and finally invalided out.

Even then he remained in London, eager to help England's
cause if he could. It was there while contacting the Ministry
of Information on some propaganda project or other that he
came across the stories of Flying Officer X., for which he at

once evinced an enormous admiration. As a result he made it his business to get to know me and then when we met declared, and in no uncertain terms, that the stories were not only admirable in themselves but that unquestionably they ought to be filmed. (That brilliant photographer, Robert Capa, who was later killed in Korea, had already made a similarly emphatic declaration about one of the stories that had come out of Oakington, *The Young Man from Kalgoorlie*, but nothing definite was ever done in that direction). Fenton was more practical. He proposed to make certain of the stories into films himself; if this came about would I write the scripts? I had never attempted a film script in my life and perhaps a little unwisely I said that I would.

One story that had much impressed Fenton was the very first I had ever written at Oakington, *It's Just the Way It Is*, in which the parents of a pilot who had been killed pay a visit to his Wing-Commander, as was the habit of parents, half to satisfy themselves that their son is really dead, half in the touching hope that he may still be alive after all. It was this story that Fenton wanted to film and I not only duly wrote the script for it but even took part in the picture, making my one and only appearance as a film actor in the guise of a dead navigator being carried on a stretcher from a shot-up bomber.

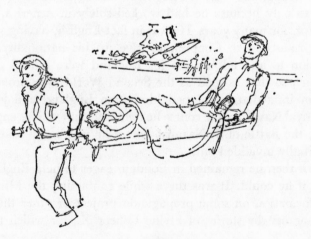

It was during this brief collaboration on the little film that Fenton suggested I must meet Sir Alexander Korda. I knew that Korda and my agent, Laurence Pollinger, had often been in association, and I readily agreed. Accordingly Fenton and I went along one afternoon to Korda's office in Piccadilly, Fenton having explained that Korda was building up a strong pool of writers for a new programme of films and that it was not improbable that he might ask me to be one of them.

But if I had any fond idea that Korda would immediately broach the subject of films and writing for them I was to be swiftly disillusioned. I found Korda a shrewd, cultivated, clever and amusing man and it was utterly in character that afternoon that instead of getting down to the practical business of talking films he immediately launched out on a discourse, hilarious as any Chaplin film, on the subject of farting.

'Ah! you know, Bates,' he said in the strong Hungarian accent he never lost and indeed probably carefully cultivated, 'I adore ze fart. I absolutely adore ze fart. Ze fart is *marvellous*. You know, Bates, what they call it in France? No? *Le piano du pauvre homme*. The poor man's piano. *Marvellous*.'

The eventual result of that inconsequential afternoon was that Korda put me under contract to him at a salary that looked phenomenal enough on paper until you woke up to the stark fact that, thanks to tax, all you got out of every pound was sixpence. There are, however, other desirable dividends in life rather than money and in this case I eagerly reached out simply in order to profit from a new experience. But one other desirable dividend that in due course presented itself was that I was able to meet, through Korda, David Lean.

David as a film director is dedicated to the proposition, as I also am as a writer, that it is the business of the artist to entertain, not to instruct, to give pleasure, not to preach morals. To this end he was extracting, or was about to extract, every ounce of entertainment from *Oliver Twist* and *Great Expectations*, as he was later to extract even more of it from *The Bridge on the River Kwai* and *Doctor Zhivago*.

David is an intense and dedicated man and we instantly got

on well together. He was quick to confess much admiration not only for some of my novels and longer stories such as *Fair Stood the Wind For France*, *The Cruise of the Breadwinner* and *The Purple Plain*, but also for many of the very short ones, the little pictorial sketches in which all is 'implied rather than chronicled', in which there is no time for 'facts, explanation and analysis'. I in turn admired his own methods, a supreme example of which is the dramatic and terrifying cut to the face of the convict in the graveyard in *Great Expectations*, a stroke of arresting shock which tells more in a split second than many a novelist, ambling discursively along, could tell in a page.

Soon David was extending his enthusiasm into more practical form by buying the film rights of *Fair Stood the Wind For France*, *The Cruise of the Breadwinner* and *The Purple Plain*, only one of which, *The Purple Plain*, has ever reached the screen. This fact has never mattered to me; the experience of the association with David was rich enough in itself and the more I saw of him and his methods the more sure I was that Coppard, in his contention that the story writer could learn much from the cinema, was right. This contention obliquely gets the blessing of Lord David Cecil, who in an introduction to a recent anthology of modern short stories has written: 'The "plot" form is a limited form and one which excludes the work of some of the greatest masters of the *genre*, from Chekhov downwards. Anyway, partly under Chekhov's influence and partly from a general loosening up of fictional form, the old convention gradually lost its grip; and by the turn of the century the short-story writer was free to shape his inspiration into what form he pleased. This is why the twentieth century is the great period for the English short story.' Exactly; nor do I think I am exaggerating when I maintain that the cinema has had some part in the evolution of that greatness.

One day, when David and I were having preparatory discussions as to what sort of boat *The Breadwinner* should be when it came to making the film, he suddenly seemed to go

off into a day-dream. When he finally emerged from it he surprised me by asking:

'Have you ever been to Tahiti?'

I confessed I never had.

'Would you like to go?'

I replied that I had always wanted to go to Tahiti. The association with Gauguin and his friends had always fascinated me.

'But why,' I said, 'are you asking me?'

In reply he went on to say that an actor friend of his had just come back from the Friendly Islands, bringing with him some excellent photographs, not only of Tahiti itself but more particularly of the island of Moorea, which lies some eighteen or twenty miles away. The photographs, when produced, showed Moorea to be an island looking very much like a piece of the Dolomites turned tropical. It also looked simple, remote and romantic, with palms restful on the shores of a placid lagoon, palm-thatched huts, high tranquil white clouds.

David asked if I didn't think it looked fascinating and I replied that there was no doubt it did.

'Would you like to go?' he said. 'You caught the atmosphere of Burma so well that I thought you might capture something of the Pacific too. I thought if you could wander around and pick up an idea for a story I'd like to make a film of it. What do you say?'

I decided it was an opportunity too good to miss. I agreed to go. This was simple enough; the problem was to know how to get there. It turned out that a boat from Marseilles took a month, a proposition which had no appeal for either Madge or me. The only possible way was by air and this, since the jet age had not begun, meant a series of long hops via New York, San Francisco, Honolulu, Fiji, Samoa, the Cook Islands and then Tahiti – Tahiti being the end of the line, with no communication with the west coast of South America.

The prospect seemed not only inviting but positively exciting and Madge and I immediately began to make preparations to go.

'It looks,' I said to David, as we pored over the photographs again, 'like a proper Lotus Land.' Perhaps I was thinking at that moment of Pierre Loti, the 19th century French writer who, like Gauguin, had fallen deeply under the spell of Polynesia. Then, recalling the painful surprise India had had in store for me I said on reflection: 'Well, we shall see.'

Lotus Land? Yes. It all depended, of course, on what you meant by Lotus Land.

Westward from New York to San Francisco, that pleasantest of cities washed by the cold waters of the North Pacific; then a long, long haul to Honolulu, with a brief call in the middle of the night at Canton Island, an Anglo-U.S. condominium with a sign-post in the middle of its white barren expanse of rock and sand proclaiming that everywhere in the world was, as I remember it, 12,000 miles away – a proclamation that induced a lowering of the spirits and a chilling sense of isolation; then eventually to Honolulu, to drive from the airport to the hotel through avenues of little stalls selling *leis* made of flowers in every conceivable brilliance of colour, and seeing on the streets girls of such beauty, many of them a cross between Chinese and Polynesian, that they are surely the prettiest in the world, and then out on the ocean itself a great white spouting of whales; and then presently on to Fiji, with Suva, the capital, full of the scent of frangipani and as hotly steaming as Calcutta itself; and then on to Samoa.

'This,' I had said to Madge as we flew on over bluer and bluer waters, 'is the way to travel. Nothing like a flying-boat. Especially the landing. You'll love the landing.'

I began to regret the words as we started to lose height over

Samoa and below us the formerly bluest of seas suddenly
became an ugly, sinister charge of white horses. A few minutes
later we were landing on a sea like a maelstrom, in a twenty-
five mile an hour crosswind, very close to peril.

'Landing?' Madge said. 'I'm glad you said landing. Oh!
yes, I loved the landing.'

'Any landing,' I reminded her, 'is a good landing.'

Rain fell in warm, steaming torrents. A number of pregnant
Polynesian women moaned with fright as the launch took us
precariously from flying-boat to anchorage and then continued
to sit huddled in fear as the bus drove us on our long journey
across the flooded island.

But even under rain Samoa looked incomparably beautiful.
It is an island of great lushness, of wooded mountains and
ravines, of many churches of all sizes and denominations (the
work of the London Missionary Society), of delightful village
greens, all looking as smooth-shaven and green as any in
England, all deliciously embroidered with many flowers, all
surrounded by big palm-thatched houses looking like circular

sea-side band-stands. On one of these greens numbers of small boys were playing cricket, totally oblivious of the torrential rain, using the central rib of a big palm frond as a bat. On another a pretty Samoan girl stood laughingly washing her naked breasts, 'the colour of dark honey', in the rain. All along the sea-coast, a short distance from the shore and joined to it by wooden gangways, stood little huts, on the purpose of which I pondered in vain until suddenly I saw the door of one of them open, to reveal a Samoan woman placidly sitting there on the loo, a sight that woke even the fear-struck pregnant women to laughter.

Apia, above which stands Vailima, the former home of Robert Louis Stevenson, looked utterly dismal under the rain, its harbour showing here and there the gaunt bones of wrecks, its waters half-grey, half-red from soil washed down from the mountains. The waterfront itself looked like something out of Somerset Maugham – indeed it was the perfect setting for his story *Rain* – or Conrad: seedy, shabby, the twilit back-end-of-nowhere, inspiring thoughts of beachcombers getting drunk in bars, except that, as we presently discovered as we wound up at our so-called hotel, there was nothing to get drunk on.

My forethought in buying a few miniature bottles of gin on the flying-boat helped us through an evening dismal with rain, black hordes of flies on the dinner table and some of the most appalling food I have ever been faced with. All night the rain pelted down and we could only pray it would stop by morning.

It did not stop. At breakfast we knew that, with the wind still raging, we were imprisoned for another day. What on earth could we do with ourselves? The answer came from a pleasant Liberian girl working on the island as a schoolteacher. Perhaps we might care to see the school? She assured us it would be interesting.

More in desperation than anything else we accepted her invitation. At the school a big class of small Samoan children sang lustily for us, the chief items of their *repertoire* being, as I

remember it, *Rule Britannia* and *London Bridge is Falling Down*.
After this we were invited to the staff mid-morning coffee,
during which someone inquired if I too was teaching. When
I said 'No, writing,' an essay in detective work began. A few
moments later someone deduced that I was the author of
The Purple Plain and a rumble of curiosity reverberated through
the teaching staff. This led to the imperative suggestion that
we must of course meet the High Commissioner. A meeting
must be arranged forthwith.

That evening we sat in the drawing-room at Vailima, the
long white timber house standing on the hills above Apia,
then the residence of the High Commissioner, formerly the
home of R.L.S., the decaying centre of the strangest of *ménages*,
where he lived for the last four years of his life. As we sat there

Robert
Louis Stevenson

talking with the Commissioner and his wife, two very pleasant
people, rain still fell torrentially outside and the air, as in one
of Stevenson's own stories, 'smelt strong of wild lime and vanilla'.
Throughout the damp, hot evening, in a temperature of
ninety degrees or so, the scene was dominated by a portrait

of the brooding, sickly, Gauguin-like figure of Stevenson himself, hypnotic, compelling, uncomfortable and by no means unsinister as it stared down from the wall: yet another example of the European artist from the cool north who had found it impossible to resist the enchantments of tropical lands and southern seas.

After another day of black hordes of flies and hopelessly bad food – the only other hotel on the waterfront was reputedly nothing but a whore-house – we flew off at last on the brightest of mornings to the Cook Islands, where big handsome Polynesian girls with long blue-black hair swam in the crystal waters of the calmest of lagoons at Atutaki, or lazed on the brilliant, almost snow-white coral sand.

The fortnightly arrival of the flying-boat at Papeete was evidently always an excuse for a near festival: crowds of gay Polynesian girls on the waterfront wearing purple and pink and white and scarlet *leis*, more *leis* for incoming travellers, a general air of care-free excitement. (I use the word care-free advisedly but will qualify it presently.) A good proportion of the girls, I was assured, were waiting for someone to sleep with, regardless of whatever price they might subsequently have to pay. The girls of Tahiti are in fact very free with their favours, to which may be added that they see no stigma of any kind in having children out of wedlock, indeed rather the reverse, since they are very fond of children and also because unions between Polynesian and Polynesian tend to be unfruitful, whereas the Polynesian female tends to become extremely fertile when mated to French, English, American, New Zealand or Australian men or almost any male except their own. The Friendly Islands would seem, indeed, to be aptly named.

Papeete itself turned out to be a scruffy little port, again half like something out of Maugham or Conrad, half like a French provincial town hopelessly gone to seed. Its shops were mostly Chinese; its bars seemed little more than brothels. Its shabby, seedy air was however greatly heightened by many flowers, most exquisite among them that loveliest of vines, the allamanda, whose butter-pure trumpets trailed with prodigal splendour everywhere. On everything there lay a great air of lassitude, of *mañana*, a feeling of 'why today? – tomorrow will do', so that it took almost all morning to cash a cheque at the old-fashioned French-like bank.

Towards the end of the 19th century a great influx of indentured labour, mostly Indian and Chinese, flooded into the Pacific, with remarkable results to be seen everywhere today. In Fiji, for example, Indians already strongly outnumber Fijians. The Melanesians, physically strong and powerful as they are, have been overtaken by Indians with their renowned merchant skills and a religion which continuously teaches and preaches fertility. These Indians today are a magnificent, prosperous people beside whom Calcutta's pavement-dossing hordes look like scum and even many Fijians look sad and heavy with the indolence which has let them become outnumbered. In Tahiti it is the Chinese who have been notably industrious, so that they are now the shop-keepers, the fishermen, the landowners, the market-gardeners. Hard-working, skilful, thrifty, they leave the Polynesians as far behind as the Indians have left the Melanesians.

The Polynesians are, in fact, a dying race. Their tendency not to reproduce among themselves is naturally largely responsible for this, but with this goes the sad fact that unions between Polynesian women and outsiders are not only highly fruitful but also productive of children who are very often mentally brilliant. This in turn is another melancholy source of frustration, since the outlook for such brilliance in Papeete is highly limited and the Sorbonne is far, far away. A schoolmaster sadly gave us an example of this, swearing that in a school painting competition ninety per cent of the winning entries, all brilliant, came from descendants of Gauguin.

But if Papeete was shabby, seedy, sad and sunk in apathy, the Pacific was certainly not. It is an Everest among oceans: vast, haunting, restless, dominating. Few areas of the world can give off such a powerful impression of being, in the strangest way, the surviving fragment of a mysterious and long-lost world. Over it broods not only that peculiar fatalistic air of coiled-up violence that is an inevitable part of all tropical atmosphere, but a high-charged feeling that at any moment a vast electric spark may leap across it and set its slumbering dramas burning and quivering. You get the same feeling when a shark explodes from the water, a dramatic slash of sinister power, a feeling that anything may happen here.

Soon, in Papeete, we found ourselves in close friendship with a congenial American doctor. We had in fact met him earlier on the flying-boat, where he had asked me to look after a wooden box for him. He said something about 'precious cargo' and when I inquired what this might be, replied 'Mosquitoes'. They were in fact a particular brand of giant mosquito apparently having the ability, like fleas on the backs of lesser fleas and so *ad infinitum*, to prey on lesser mosquitoes. The American in fact was engaged in research into the disease filariasis, formerly better known as elephantiasis. Filariasis is perhaps the least aesthetic of many unaesthetic tropical diseases, turning the limbs, even of young girls, into hideous elephantine lumps of swollen flesh that are distressing to behold. The disease is carried by mosquitoes, in a cycle as simple as it is sinister. It begins with a coconut falling from a tree. It continues with a rat gnawing a hole in the coconut, then with rain, which falls with fair frequency in Tahiti, filling up the coconut. In the stagnant rainwater mosquitoes breed, subsequently flying off to bite first of all some sufferer from filariasis and then someone who hasn't got filariasis but soon will have. The lymphatic glands having thus been impregnated, the cycle is all ready to begin again via coconut, rat, rain and all.

It was the American doctor's hope that the resident mosquito population might be much reduced, if not wiped out, by his imported giants. In due course he took us along to his research laboratory to see his mosquito menagerie and then to hospital to see some of the mosquito's distressful victims. He had, however, other weapons in his armoury besides the imported giants. These were largely pills and one afternoon he invited me to tour some parts of the island with him, so that I could see for myself another side of his work.

'But not Madge,' he said.

'No? Why not?'

'I don't think this,' he said, 'is for Madge.'

We motored along the black-sanded shore – the beaches in Tahiti are all of black sand, looking very much like a foundry yard – past the sinister fallen coconuts, past the house reputed to have been lived in by Gauguin, past other houses at which the doctor honked on the car-horn in order to give a passing signal to a friend ('No reply. Ah! it's three o'clock. Guess he's in bed with his *vahini*'), until at last we reached a little bay. Some distance inland was a small market-garden growing lettuces, radishes, carrots, water-cress and so on. In a wretched hovel, which stank like the sewer it probably was, a Chinaman and his wife were packing and washing vegetables. The Chinaman's method was to wash his feet and the vegetables in the same water, at the same time. The air was odious with stench; and I now understood why this was not for Madge.

Presently the doctor was speaking to the Chinaman. The Chinaman made gestures of innocent protest. The doctor spoke again. The Chinaman pointed towards the sea.

'What,' I said, 'is it all about?'

'The taking of pills. The artful bastards know a thousand and one tricks to make you believe they've taken them when they never have. They hold them under the tongue, in the cheek, anything. This one hasn't taken his because he's going fishing tonight and he says the pills will make him sick and he'll fall overboard. His wife hasn't taken hers because apparently the stars are not right.'

'Pure superstition.'

'Superstition, pure or otherwise, we have always with us.'

The Chinaman paddled his filthy legs and feet in water containing water-cress. I retched and was nearly sick.

'The Lotus Land,' I said.

'What was that? What did you say?'

'Nothing much. I was merely thinking,' I said, 'of the Lotus Land.'

XII

The casual nature of life in Tahiti was well illustrated a few days later when we were suddenly told by a man who kept one of the town's better bars:

'Oh! by the way, the Larsens are expecting you for the week-end.'

'The Larsens? Who are the Larsens?'

'American couple. They live on Moorea. Dying to meet you.'

I inquired as to how we got to Moorea.

'Schooner. Goes every morning at 9.30. You're expected Saturday. Be down on the waterfront soon after 9.'

On Saturday morning we duly arrived on the waterfront soon after 9. The front was crowded with the usual throng of Tahitians madly doing nothing but there was, as far as I could see, nothing in sight that could be called a schooner. We idled about for half an hour or so, I with growing impatience, until suddenly Madge drew my attention to what seemed to be a large white ramshackle barrel sawn in half and moored to the quay-side. This was being loaded with cargo, bicycles, casks of wine, people and even a horse, the animal being eventually strapped to the side of the deck. This, it turned out, was our schooner.

We went aboard. Several women passengers, as if in anticipation of terrors to come, appeared already to have given up the ghost and lay immobile on deck or on seats with their heads completely covered with shawls. The horse didn't look particularly tranquil either. Of captain and crew there was no sign but more and more cargo, people, wine and bicycles kept coming aboard.

Ten o'clock came and went but still no crew. By this time the morning was already hotting up and the air was thick and sickening with the smell of engine oil. There is invariably a vast swell on the surface of the Pacific and I began to suffer inwardly for Madge, who isn't the best of sailors. Now and then one of the prostrate covered women would give a stifled groan and the horse, growing more restless, would nervously stamp its hooves on the deck.

When eleven o'clock came I was in a mood to disembark and find ourselves a long cool drink somewhere. At this moment a huge, tipsy-looking Tahitian with one eye stumbled aboard, followed by two disreputable characters in no better state, each carrying a bottle of wine. This, I judged, was our captain and crew and my sympathies were now firmly with the moaning, covered women.

Presently one of the crew opened up a hatchway and disappeared into a black hole below decks. The captain took the wheel in one hand and an uncorked bottle of wine in the other and after a sudden shattering explosion from the black hole below decks we were ready to sail into the hot, blinding white light of the great open Pacific. With a certain trepidation I then remembered that although the journey was a mere eighteen miles or so in distance it was to take four hours or more in time.

The swell on the ocean was vast. The barrel perilously rolled, pitched and ducked. Except for an occasional groan or two the covered women might have been dead. The only persons unperturbed were the captain and crew, who swigged with relish and regularity at the wine bottles, at the same time breaking into loud vinous laughter. This gave One-eye an incongruously leering look, as if he were positively enjoying the tribulations of his wretched passengers. By this time we could see Moorea, jagged against the skyline, and the schooner seemed more than ever like a lump of white, drifting flotsam as it pitched and rolled towards the wall of dark rocks.

About this time I discovered that someone had left a Paris newspaper – which one I now forget – on one of the deck seats. Ever anxious to improve my halting French I seized upon it eagerly and spent the next half hour or so reading columns of those fascinating advertisements, always more beguiling in French than in English, in which lonely persons of both sexes proffer their charms and statistics in a yearning search for a mate. By now most of the women were not dead but horrifically and loudly seasick and I have never been so glad of a newspaper in my life.

Soon, to my undisguised relief, I heard the engine cut out and I looked up to realize that we were drifting in towards an anchorage under the high, palm-clad rocks. When we were finally tied up by a jetty there was an eager rush of passengers to lay hands on great frosty chunks of pink and amber water-melon being sold on the quay. While these were being consumed there was a vigorous unloading of cargo and wine-barrels.

We, having no local currency, were unable to buy any water-melon, but presently one of the crew leapt ashore and came back with two delicious amber hunks, into which we buried our faces eagerly, at the same time staring into the depths of crystal-bright water at vast and brilliant shoals of tropical fish in every sort of colour from dazzling electric blue to vivid yellow, an astonishing fishy kaleidoscope flashing this way and that with ordered speed, the whole thing looking as if freshly painted.

This was the first of three stops at similar anchorages along the coast-line and at each of them the pattern of water-melon, rolling wine-barrels and the kaleidoscope of fish was repeated. We came at last to the entrance to a big lagoon with the inevitable coral reef guarding the entrance and offering a barrier to the Pacific, whose gigantic waves charged it constantly like a massed attack of mad, white-maned fighting horses. There is something fearful about this savage and primeval conflict between ocean wave and coral reef and I never watched it without a certain chill of fright.

After the lash and roar of this ocean conflict the inner reaches of the lagoon were almost deathly quiet. We glided smoothly along between walls of palm and hibiscus and allamanda and frangipani, drifting quietly for perhaps two miles, perhaps more, until we could see at last the head of the lagoon, with houses, a cluster of fishing boats and another anchorage.

As we pulled into this we saw, among the little crowd gathered on the jetty, a middle-aged man and woman waving enthusiastically. Anticipating that these were the Larsens we waved back.

They were indeed the Larsens and soon, on shore, we were being welcomed like long-lost relations, returning prodigals or bosom friends. It was not until some long time later that we learned that the Larsens had not the remotest clue as to our identity. They didn't even know our names. They had simply invited us out of an eager hunger for contact with someone from the world beyond the boundaries of the Lotus Land.

Moorea is one of the most beautiful islands in the world; few places can lay a firmer claim to the word paradise. Not only is this pictorially so but the Larsens, on their estate of 4000 acres, were self-sufficient in everything but wine. From oranges to coffee, bananas to fresh-water shrimps, beef to vanilla, chickens to lemons, timber to fish: theirs could truly be called a land flowing with milk and honey.

Their house was roomy but unpretentious, set in a rambling garden of palms, tree ferns, bananas, hibiscus, frangipani and ginger lilies. We ourselves were assigned to a big bare wooden hut that Madge insists was more like an isolation hospital than a house. My own recollection is that it was hot and uncomfortable and that the constant crowing of jungle cocks kept us awake half the night.

In the morning we breakfasted on coffee so exquisite of flavour and aroma that I was inspired to a chorus of praise for it, even going so far as to say that I felt I was really drinking coffee for the first time in my life. It was purest nectar. The Larsens explained its secret: it came, first of all, from the estate; not a single bean, in the second place, was roasted or ground until it was seven years old – coffee beans apparently having the virtue, like wine or sardines, of improving with age; and last, only the essential quantity needed for each day was roasted and ground at any one time. Certainly, neither before nor since, have I tasted coffee of such ethereal quality.

After breakfast we wandered about the estate. Much of it was hilly, all of it lush. 'The air,' as Stevenson had once written, 'smelt strong of wild lime and vanilla'. This was scarcely surprising, since vanilla, which is an orchid, (*Vanilla planifolia*), was growing everywhere: soft cream lady-slipper flowers of great delicacy giving off their slightly heady scent. During the war synthetic vanilla had largely replaced natural vanilla until it was discovered that the synthetic product might be a possible cause of cancer; as a result natural vanilla was again in demand and that morning on the hillside among giant banana trees *petite* Chinese women were hand-fertilising vanilla flowers, which are self-sterile, doing the required work with a matchstick, their delicate fingers so swift that they could fertilise a possible two thousand flowers a day. The resulting vanilla pod takes about six months to mature and then resembles a tobacco-brown bean which, incidentally, may be usefully kept with your coffee beans to give them a subtle aromatic flavour.

As we watched the Chinese women deftly engaged among the vanilla flowers it suddenly began to rain torrentially. The air steamed; it was as if we were in a warm sticky bath as we ran for shelter in a little wooden hut. The rain ceased as swiftly as it had begun, leaving the jungle of vines and palms and bananas and tree-ferns and bamboo dripping and sparkling. As we walked back down the hillside we stopped to pick oranges from a tree, and to the air that 'smelt strong of wild lime and vanilla' was suddenly added the rich fragrance of the oil of orange peel.

Next morning we walked in an opposite direction, along the shores of the lagoon, on a dry stony track that wound through high palms. We had scarcely started when once again it began to rain torrentially. This time there was no hut in which to shelter and we were obliged to walk on, again as in a warm sticky bath, until we were soaked to the skin. There was nothing to worry about in this. We simply walked on until the rain abruptly stopped and the sun came out, immediately hot and sparkling, the palm fronds dripping a great spattering cascade of silver raindrops. Then we found a stretch of sand on the lagoon shore, in full sun, and there took off our clothes and hung them to dry on a bush while we lay naked in the sun and rolled in the tepid shallow water. This, for an hour or so, was truly the Lotus Land.

The strong attraction which islands have for man is one I find of endless fascination. Men long to possess islands as they long to possess lovers. There are never enough islands, it would seem, to satisfy man's great island appetite. Yet John dos Passos, the American novelist, hit on a singular truth when he described Madeira, his birthplace, as 'very lovely but a prison, a beautiful prison'. What is true of Madeira is even more true of Tahiti and Moorea and as many islands of the Pacific as you care to name. What attracted Stevenson and Loti and Gauguin and his several friends to them? No doubt a means of escape from something – but an escape to what? Dos Passos, it seems to me, had the answer – nothing more than an escape to prison.

The Larsens were another illustration of this. Their beautiful paradise, rich, lush, peaceful, self-sufficient, its infinite natural beauties amazingly and dramatically enhanced every evening by what must be the most spectacular sunsets in the world – it is exactly as if the lid of a giant cauldron is suddenly lifted across the ocean, filling the sky with flame, orange, scarlet, yellow, rose and richest purple until the eyes themselves almost burn too as they try to absorb its powerful intensity – was really a prison which caused one to recall another truth, namely that of Sir John Suckling, who reminded us long ago that 'stone walls do not a prison make, nor iron bars a cage'. No: the paradise of a Lotus lagoon deep in the Pacific can create prison just as successfully – so that when I think of the Larsens it is not so much with a memory of their exquisite coffee, the delicious flavour of fresh-water shrimps or the air strong with 'wild lime and vanilla', as with a picture of them, in the days before flying-boats revolutionized communications, sitting down at breakfast every morning and going through the solemn ritual of opening a newspaper that the monthly boat from Marseilles had brought. That the paper was a month old was of no importance. It was an infinitely precious link from prison to the outside world.

Before we left Moorea one other thing seemed to me to symbolize the illusion that here was paradise. We were again walking along the shore of the lagoon when we came upon a tree, a species of hibiscus. This is not the hibiscus which provides the glorious saucers of pink and scarlet and yellow that Polynesian girls wear in their hair but an altogether taller tree whose bark provides the material from which so-called grass-skirts are made. An interesting characteristic of this hibiscus is that its flowers, more like bells than saucers, begin the day by being white, then turn creamy-yellow by noon and then a sort of cloudy crimson by sunset, when they at last fall off, their brief daily cycle of blossoming finished. Beautiful and ephemeral, that tree has ever since seemed to me to symbolize the Polynesian *malaise*.

The week-end being over, we took the schooner back to Papeete and then, a week later, left Papeete too. I wasn't sad to leave the sadness of Tahiti, a sadness made deeper by an incident of a character I later weaved into a story called *Mrs Eglantine*.

'Every morning Mrs Eglantine sat at the round bamboo bar of the New Pacific Hotel and drank her breakfast. This consisted of two quick large brandies, followed by several slower ones. By noon breakfast had become lunch and by two o'clock the pouches under and above Mrs Eglantine's bleared blue eyes had begun to look like large puffed pink prawns.'

'I suppose you know you've got her name wrong?' my friend the doctor said to me. 'It's really Eglinton. What makes you call her Eglantine?'

'She must have been rather sweet at some time.'

'You think so?' he said. 'What has Eglantine got to do with that?'

'The Sweet-briar,' I said, 'or the Vine, or the twisted Eglantine.'

Mrs Eglantine was in fact a piece of alcoholic flotsam such as Maugham and Conrad were fond of describing. She at least had no illusions about the Paradise and the Lotus Land:

Mrs Eglantine

'Swindle. The big myth. The great South-sea bubble. The great South-sea paradise. Not a decent hotel in the place. All the shops owned by Chinks. Everybody bone-lazy. Takes you all day to cash a cheque at the bank. Hot and dirty . . . You've seen the travel posters, haven't you, dear? Those nice white sands and the Polynesian girls with naked bosoms climbing the palms. All a myth, dear. All a bloody swindle. All taken in the Cook Islands, hundreds of miles away.'

Mrs Eglantine had other sources of disillusionment and bitterness. She had come all the way from Australia to marry a Frenchman in Tahiti only to find, on arrival, that the Administration had posted him, in her view deliberately, to New Caledonia. Her dilemma now was that she was either waiting permission to stay on the island, or deportation – she didn't know which. She was bitter too with the French, who didn't like the British, and further embittered by the Governor, who didn't like her. 'Undesirable type, dear. Divorced and drinks too much. Bad combination.'

Eventually it turned out that Mrs Eglantine was to be deported and it happened that she flew out on the same flying-boat as we did. She was much depressed and I bought her customary breakfast for her on the plane. The irony of her going was that she had to be deported to the nearest British possession, which happened to be the Cook Islands, which under a system of partial prohibition were virtually dry. It was hard to know what Mrs Eglantine would have for breakfast.

At Atutaki, after the flying-boat had landed on the lagoon and was being re-fuelled, a group of Polynesian women and girls were singing songs of farewell to a young man about to leave on the plane.

'The songs of Polynesia have a great sadness in them. A few of the women were weeping. Then at the last moment a girl rushed on bare feet along the jetty towards the waiting launch, wringing her hands in sorrow, her long hair flying, bitterly weeping final words of good-bye.

'On the scalding white coral beach, under the palms, there was no sign of Mrs Eglantine. And presently, as the launch moved away, I could no longer hear the songs of sad farewell or the haunting voice of the girl who was weeping. But only, running through my head, haunting too:

' "The Sweet-briar, or the Vine, or the twisted Eglantine".'

XIII

During the war and in the years immediately after it I had travelled much and far. I had seen the squalor, the fatalism and the charm of India, the ruin and grace of Burma, the colonial piracy of the Bahamas, something of the West Indies and America, something of the Middle East, from the Pyramids to the great wondrous towers of Baalbek, much of Europe and a glimpse, an unaffectionate glimpse, of the Far North. But wherever I went, and however far, I was for ever left with one unbreakable, unshakeable conviction: there was, for me, among the wonders, the paradises, the Lotus Lands and all, no place like England. The more my world enlarged and ripened the more English I became.

At the heart of all this lay an odd paradox. Whenever I began to think in terms of a novel I could conceive of no other background than my native Midlands, the valleys of my childhood which I had left many years before. The powerful knot which bound me to them refused to be broken. Ardent lover of the south country and, in particular Kent, though I had become, consistently maintaining that here was some of the loveliest countryside in the land, I felt no kind of urge to place a novel there. Short stories and *novellas*, yes, but never a longer work. To complete the paradox I no longer felt impelled to place a shorter work in the county of my childhood.

Somewhere in the mid-fifties, however, I began restlessly nursing a new idea. I had long been fascinated by a rural junk-yard I used to pass two or three times a week. Its crazy mess of old iron, rusting implements, pigs, horses, geese, turkeys, haystacks and useless junk of every kind sat incongruously next to the most beautiful of bluebell woods, the junk mocking the beauty, the bluebells mocking the junk. Here, it seemed to me, was something that had to be written about. The more I thought about it, however,

147

the farther I seemed to get from any kind of accomplishment.

Here, in fact, was the perfect example of a negative needing a positive to wake it to life. I did not, however, go round consciously searching for a positive; experience teaches that these things happen by accident, unexpectedly. And so it was. One early summer evening Madge and I were driving through a Kentish village twenty-five miles east of us, in apple orchard country, when she suddenly had reason to stop and make a few purchases at the village shop. As I sat waiting for her in the car I noticed, outside the shop, a ramshackle lorry that had been recently painted a violent electric blue. Two or three minutes later there came out of the shop, in high spirits, a remarkable family: father a perky, sprightly character with dark side-burnings, Ma a youngish handsome woman of enormous girth, wearing a bright salmon jumper and shaking with laughter like a jelly, and six children, the eldest of them a beautiful dark-haired girl of twenty or so. All were sucking at colossal multi-coloured ice-creams and at the same time crunching potato crisps. As they piled into the lorry there was an air of gay and uninhibited abandon about it all. Wild laughter rang through the village street and the whole scene might have come out of Merrie England.

This, I suddenly knew, was my positive; here were the inhabitants of my junk-yard. Next morning, in a fever of excitement and laughter, I set the family going in a short story called *The Darling Buds of May*, in which the unconventional natures of Pop, Ma and their children are unashamedly revealed. The eldest and most beautiful girl, unmarried, is revealed as being pregnant, but exactly by whom she doesn't know. Does it matter? Not on your life – 'perfick', says Pop. He, the junkdealer, his pockets stuffed with fat rolls of pound notes, is revealed as never paying income tax. He regards it as sort of immoral even to think of doing so. The entire family is gargantuan of appetite, unenslaved by conventions, blissfully happy. Pop is further revealed as a passionate lover of the countryside, as ardent a worshipper at the bluebell shrine and its nightingales as he is of Ma's seductive, voluptuous

bosoms. He yields to no man in his warm, proud love of England. All is 'perfick'.

Presently it seemed to me a thousand pities to confine such a rich gallery of characters to a short story. In their lusty love of life they cried out for greater space, richer pastures. I accordingly began to expand them into a novel. The Larkin household was then revealed in all its uninhibited glory: two enormous television sets, a Rolls-Royce, a vast glittering cocktail cabinet from which Pop dispenses cocktails of a terrifying potency with such names as Red Bull and Rolls-Royce, a potency that affects Mr Charlton, a visiting tax-man, with dire consequences. His seduction by Mariette being at last complete, he finds himself surrendering completely to the Larkins, the Larkin household and above all the Larkin philosophy, which is all *carpe diem* and the very antithesis of the Welfare State. The Larkins' secret is in fact that they live as many of us would like to live if only we had the guts and nerve to flout the conventions. Pop and Ma demonstrate that they have the capacity by indulging deeply in love and champagne before breakfast, passion in the bluebell wood and encouraging their enchanting daughter to a life of wilful seduction. Ma too has a philosophy all her own. It is what she calls 'lending Pop out'. Thoroughly aware of Pop's attraction for the opposite sex, and *vice versa*, she has no compunction whatever about letting him have an occasional fling with others, whether beautiful or, like the spinster Miss Pilchester, merely hungry and unsatisfied. Result: much Chaucerian fun and infinite happiness.

The Darling Buds of May was instantly a phenomenal success. It went into many languages. Colonials and Americans, having tended to think of the English as cold stuffed-shirts, seized upon its wanton, Chaucerian joys, its flouting of conventions and the Welfare State, with joy and relish. It also became revealed as a healer of the sick, a blower away of the blues. From all quarters came reports of laughter killing depression, of the Larkins working miracles in hospital wards. An American woman wrote to say that one day on looking out of her window she was much startled to see her next-door neighbour writhing on her bed in the throes of apparent agony. On rushing to her aid she found that it was nothing of the kind; she was merely reading *The Darling Buds of May*.

Thus encouraged, I proceeded to a second novel, *A Breath of French Air*, in which the entire Larkin family, new baby and all, set off in the Rolls-Royce for a French holiday, only to suffer certain disillusionments in the matter of French weather, French food ('We shan't get very fat on this') and French sanitary arrangements. The whole thing develops into a wanton Bacchanale. From this I proceeded still further to *When the Green Woods Laugh, Oh! to be in England* and finally to *A Little of What you Fancy*, not the least distinctive feature of which is the behaviour of Primrose, the beautiful archseductress who is not only capable of thinking, in true Larkin fashion, through the pores of her skin but also proves she is capable of a double act by openly seducing the local curate with her voluptuous body in a mushroom field, having first softened him up with even more voluptuous quotations on the subject of uninhibited love from Blake and Donne.

The Larkins could, if necessary, be read on two planes: purely for the sheer joy of their enviable way of life, but also as a reflection on the revolution that had overtaken post-war England, a revolution that had nowhere been so marked as in the English countryside. In the early thirties not a single farm worker in my village had a car, many not even a bicycle; today many have two cars, many a cottage inhabited by a family displays four, five, even six cars; few village shops sold anything but mouse-trap cheese, fat bacon, candles, paraffin, tart oranges and boiled sweets; today every one has its deep freeze dispensing scampi, smoked salmon, *spaghetti bolognese* and exotics of every kind. Not that it was either essential or necessary to interpret the books as being in any way a treatise on the revolution; the point was never laboured or forced. The surface delight was no mere coating for a pill; it could be unashamedly enjoyed, as Ma and Pop unashamedly enjoyed their love and champagne and Primrose her seduction by flesh and poetry in the fields, for its own sake.

The comedian in me, which much earlier in my career had produced *My Uncle Silas* and other pieces in lighter vein, is not only capable of laughing at the foibles of others or indulging in the effervescence of comedy; it is also a source of self-criticism; it is a means of preventing myself from taking myself too seriously, of becoming pompous; it even enables me to poke fun at myself and my own short-comings.

It is not to be denied, moreover, that there is something of myself in Pop Larkin: a passionate Englishman, a profound love of Nature, of the sounds and sights of the countryside, of colour, flowers and things sensual; a hatred of pomp, pretension and humbug; a lover of children and family life; an occasional breaker of rules, a flouter of conventions. The only things I don't share with Pop are a business ability to sell junk at a profit of three hundred and more per cent or to avoid the payment of income tax.

Pop is in fact an expression of my own philosophy: the need to go with the stream, never to battle against it. The prolific fruits of this are to be seen in Pop's many children, as they are to be seen in mine. To my four, Ann, Judith, Richard and Jonathan, all now grown up, are now added progeny of their own: Stephen, Jeremy, Andrew, Beverley, Emma, Jonathan, Lydia, Timothy, Catherine and Justin. A handsome cornucopia.

As I write these final words I am looking out over the garden that, forty years ago, was a derelict farmyard; it is now rich in maturity, bright not only with autumn colour but here and there, with a mauve iris or two, a witch hazel, a viburnum in blossom, with a premature touch of spring. Beyond it stand the great turkey oaks, pure molten gold against the most tranquil of blue November skies in the morning sun. These splendid trees are, to me, something more than trees. They stand for England, my England.

In them, indeed, I see the world in ripeness. *Bon fruit*, the French say, *mûrit tard*, or if you prefer English: 'ripeness is all'.